British Farming

British Farming

Changing Policies and Production Systems

E. S. Carter and J. M. Stansfield

FARMING PRESS

First published 1994

ISBN 0 85236 278 1

A catalogue record for this book is available
from the British Library

Published by Farming Press Books
Wharfedale Road, Ipswich IP1 4LG, United Kingdom

Distributed in North America
by Diamond Farm Enterprises,
Box 537, Alexandria Bay, NY 13607, USA

Cover design by Andrew Thistlethwaite
Typeset by Galleon Photosetting, Ipswich
Printed and bound in Great Britain by
Biddles Ltd, Guildford and King's Lynn

CONTENTS

A colour section appears between pages 100 and 101

PREFACE

Much has been written and published about recent changes in the British countryside and particularly about the influence of farming practices on the landscape and wildlife.

Most of this has appeared in general terms implying that all parts of the country have experienced such activities as hedge removal on a massive scale and that so called 'prairie farming' can be seen from one end of the country to the other. Those who live and work in the countryside know that this is not true. There are very wide regional differences, and much of the countryside is well farmed, visually attractive and supports a thriving wildlife. Farmers and their families live in the countryside and they are concerned about their environment; during the last ten years over 23,500 have asked for, and acted upon, FWAG advice about wildlife and landscape conservation. Demand for such advice continues, as does the continuing public interest in farming and food production.

The public at large have a great interest in the countryside: how it is used, how food is produced and why farmers act in the ways they do. Although information is available, it is often scattered among different agencies and not always easy to obtain. Some information may even be suspect and seen as promoting special interests. Regularly updated statistical information about farming and food sets out the facts but can be cold and impersonal, however well presented. Why are fewer people employed on farms? What effect does this have on the countryside and the way in which farming is carried out? Why did oilseed rape become such a popular crop during the 1980s? What is set-aside and why do farmers have to have it? Can farmers grow crops for fuel energy rather than for food? These are some of the questions being regularly asked by consumers, who are usually also taxpayers.

Today 72% of food is purchased in large supermarkets which require regular supplies of high-quality produce and of produce which will be available all the year round, for today's consumer no longer recognises the rhythm of the seasons, although these still impinge on the producer. In order to maintain supplies, food products are sourced from large-scale producers, either here or overseas, who are able to meet the demands of the supermarket buyers. Food production, marketing and consumption is big business involving large amounts of food and a complex storage, transport and distribution system with a large capital investment.

In 1992 the Farm Management Unit at Reading University and the Centre of Management in Agriculture published 'Food – Its Production, Marketing and Consumption', edited by Hilary Marks. Jack Whelan, then running the Food and Farming Information Service, suggested that there was a need to put flesh on the bare bones of the statistics, and this we have tried to do. It is a huge subject and one which, if covered in detail, would require a very large volume. We have concentrated on the main issues and attempted to place the changes in perspective. To do this requires some background, and a glance at the past should help the reader to understand why and how we have arrived at the present.

Farming, like any other activity, is today increasingly influenced by regulations, controls and restrictions, most of them quite recent. Farmers in the past had more freedom of action but we now live in a more complicated and regulated world. The majority of the public like to feel protected from risks and, as a result, much legislation is designed and applied to minimise any risks from diseases and pests and possible contamination, in order to provide food which is as safe as it is possible to make it.

There is, too, greater public concern about, and interest in, animal welfare, both domestic and wild, and in the general care of the countryside. Rules, regulations, codes of practice, guidelines and advice proliferate. All have to be taken into account when designing farming systems as well as when planning day to day operations. The modern farmer therefore needs to be aware of all these factors. He is frequently involved in providing capital sums to modify the farm facilities in order to meet the needs of the environment – with adverse and sometimes even terminal effects on his business.

Adrian Phillips, the recently retired Director of the Countryside Commission, has stated that, at the last count, there are some 28 ways of identifying parts of our countryside or adjoining seas for special measures of conservation of landscape or wildlife. This is because our instruments of protection have grown over the years, responding to different requirements and perceived needs. All these designations are identified by acronyms and the sheer complexity creates confusion. Pity the poor farmer or landowner trying to get to grips with what looks like an alphabet soup, for many will have a direct bearing on his farming practices. It was once said that if a farmer had two sons he should have one trained in modern farming

and the other in accountancy to ensure the future success of his
farming business. Today he might be well advised to have one
trained in the law as well!

We readily acknowledge the help we have received from Hilary
Marks in updating the statistics on which we have drawn and to
many friends and colleagues for valuable assistance and comments.
The views expressed are our own. We are particularly grateful to
Sheila Smith and Barbara Reeves for typing numerous versions and
to Roger Smith, Julanne Arnold and their colleagues at Farming
Press for their invaluable help and encouragement.

E.S. Carter and J.M. Stansfield March 1994

FOREWORD

The Earl of Selborne, KBE, FRS, DL, FRAgS
Chairman of the House of Lords Select Committee on Science and Technology

For a period of some sixty years ending with the outbreak of the Second World War, agriculture in the United Kingdom was in steady decline. The area of cropped land and leys declined from about 18 million hectares in 1875 to under 11 million hectares in 1938. Land prices were lower in the 1930s than they had been in the 1860s and such new technology as was being introduced onto British farms was directed more at extensive than intensive agriculture. One forward-looking farmer, Arthur Hosier of Wiltshire, was developing milk production systems based on low cost forage and relying on mobile milking machines with electric fencing to exploit extensive areas of chalk grassland.

The severe food shortages of the war years led to totally different priorities. Each farmer was required to crop as much of his land as possible at the highest practical level of production. The research and development services were required to promote new technology for intensive production to meet highly ambitious targets. The success in meeting such targets was rightly considered a triumph for agricultural policymakers as well as for farmers themselves. After the war the fear of recurring food shortages led to the 1947 Agriculture Act, which provided the framework for a secure agricultural industry and a dramatic expansion in agricultural production.

However, only some twenty years later widespread support for this policy gave way to concern at the impact of agriculture on the countryside.

Had we not entered the EEC in the 1970s this country would not have pursued for so long the expansionist route of the Common Agriculture Policy (CAP). While farmers continued to respond to the economic incentives provided by the CAP, the wider public expressed ever-increasing concern at the cost of surpluses, at the changes to the rural landscape and at animal welfare issues arising from intensive livestock production systems.

The CAP was not reformed until 1992 and then the spur which brought about overdue changes was as much the need to bring

European agriculture into line with the requirements of the General Agreement on Tariffs and Trade (GATT) as to meet these criticisms. Farmers remain concerned that the reformed CAP does not command widespread acceptance, particularly in Great Britain. Yet if European agriculture is to survive in competition with other parts of the world there must be continued support, though not necessarily at present levels. The agricultural policies of the 1940s were successful because there was a clear understanding of what was required and what was possible. We need the benefit of equal clarity of thought today.

Eric Carter and Malcolm Stansfield have described the changes that have taken place over the last sixty years both in the policies and in the production systems of British farming. The value of this important record is that it enables the reader to appreciate the extent to which agricultural policy needs to balance the opportunities afforded by new technology and new markets with the constraints demanded by a cautious public. Yet consumers expect our production to be competitive with alternative supplies grown where constraints may be very different.

Biotechnology promises many benefits for agriculture. It will reduce our dependence on agrochemicals and will offer new vaccines with important benefits for animal health. Farmers see this new technology as a helpful weapon in reducing costs, but it will only be available if policymakers can ensure that the regulations governing its use are sufficiently robust to command widespread public confidence. If British livestock housing systems are to be modified to meet more stringent animal welfare specifications, we must not allow the import of products from systems which do not meet these standards.

We need to devise policies that assist the production of low-priced, safe food at an acceptable cost from systems which are recognised to be environmentally benign and which pay due regard to animal welfare. The authors make a valuable contribution to the debate on the nature of such policies by demonstrating how our present policies and production systems have evolved.

With a better understanding of our agricultural past we can formulate appropriate policies for the future.

SELBORNE

March 1994

CHAPTER ONE

Introduction

The story of British farming and the agricultural industry since the Second World War has been told many times and from many different points of view. To those who can remember the depression of the 1930s and the severe food shortages of the war years, it is a success story characterised by new technology being adopted and put into practice, increasing output of quality food and a prosperous and well-cared for countryside. Others, perhaps not so closely involved, regret the changes in the appearance of the countryside, the loss of some wildlife and the increasing emphasis on the farm as a business rather than a way of life. Farming, encouraged by government support and applied research disseminated by a well-organised advisory service has, perhaps, been too successful. Increased output has, in more recent years, exceeded demand, and with the major products shielded from economic forces surpluses have built up in store. Some storage is, of course, necessary as the weather still exerts a considerable influence on output and reserves are needed to balance one year with another. However, no society can contemplate storing ever-increasing quantities of major commodities indefinitely or risk upsetting international trade by selling (or dumping) the surplus. Agricultural production and farming, once regarded as a problem for individual governments or groups of countries in the European Union (EU), becomes an international problem.

Because food is an essential human need (together with a clean, wholesome supply of water), control of food supplies, at least the basic commodities, goes back a long way. The English Corn Laws, which began in the Middle Ages and ended some six centuries later in 1869, had the general aim of maintaining an abundant supply of food at fair and steady prices; of assisting the agricultural industry; of preventing rural depopulation and of making the nation independent of imported food supplies. The main effect of these Corn Laws was to stabilise prices between periods of abundance and shortage.

1

The Corn Laws were repealed in 1846 and the duties gradually modified until they ceased in 1869. For a time, as society created more wealth and living standards rose, farming prospered in what has been called its 'Golden Age'. However, improved transport and the opening up of farming in North America, Australia and elsewhere resulted in increasing amounts of wheat and meat being imported, and home farming declined to the extent that by the end of the 19th century three-quarters of the wheat consumed in Britain came from abroad, half the butter from the continent and two-thirds of the cheese from the British colonies.

Washing sheep in the stream. This would not be approved of by today's NRA inspector!

There was some improvement in the industry during the First World War and for a short time afterwards but, with the possible exception of dairy farming, the agricultural depression did not go away and was relieved only by the outbreak of the Second World War. It is ironic that the landscape of the early years of this century, for which there is so much nostalgia, was actually the direct result of agricultural depression.

Virtual free trade had resulted in very depressed farm incomes during the 1920s and 1930s, especially in arable farming. With the outbreak of the Second World War in 1939 farm incomes improved following guaranteed prices set at a level sufficiently generous to give farmers the inducement to produce more. In 1940 agricultural product prices were a third above the 1936–38 average and farm incomes the highest for a decade. Farming was tightly controlled by the War Agricultural Executive Committees during the war with the aim of increasing basic food production by all possible means. In return for guaranteed prices and markets the industry accepted controls over supplies of feeding stuffs and fertilisers, tractors and machinery and directions over what crops could be grown and livestock kept.

POST-WAR DEVELOPMENTS

After the war ended in 1945 the nation still needed greater production from our farms – food rationing did not end until 1953 – and so generous guaranteed prices were continued for the major agricultural crops and livestock products. The 1947 Agriculture Act was passed with support from all parties and stated that: 'The twin pillars upon which the Government's agricultural policy rests are stability and efficiency. The method of providing stability is through guaranteed prices and assured markets.'

Annual price reviews were instigated and prices fixed for the main crops (wheat, barley, oats, rye, potatoes and sugar beet) eighteen months ahead and minimum prices for fatstock, milk and eggs fixed for between two and four years ahead. An Agricultural Expansion Plan aimed to raise output from agriculture by 20% above its current level and 50% over pre-war, which was later raised to 60%. However world cereal prices fell in 1953 and minimum guaranteed prices were switched to deficiency payments for cereals. Later, in 1963, open-ended guarantees were replaced by standard quantities with subsidies limited to a fixed total and excess production allowed to find its own market level.

In the Agriculture Act of 1957 some long-term assurances were set out. These included an undertaking not to reduce the guaranteed price of any commodity by more than 4% in any one year, not to reduce the price of livestock or livestock products by more than 9% in total in any three consecutive years and not to reduce the total value of guarantees by more than 2.5% in any one year. Given stability in prices and long-term guarantees, farm incomes rose and farmers had the confidence to undertake capital investments and take on new technology. Arable farming did very well, as the price of cereals increased more than other commodity prices, crop yields rose through the use of new varieties, and herbicides and more fertiliser and machinery replaced labour. Income on dairy and upland farms rose more slowly as there was less scope for mechanisation. Larger farms benefited more than small ones because smaller farms were more dependent on livestock.

During the 1970s and after Britain's entry into the European Economic Community the system of price support changed from deficiency payments to protection and intervention payments. There was a complex system of monetary compensation amounts which attempted, without success, to keep farm product prices similar in different countries. Farm incomes generally remained satisfactory, at least for a time. Poor harvests in the United States and a world shortage of grain raised prices with wheat going from £34.50 a ton in 1972–73 to £58.50 a ton the following year. There was talk of world starvation. This soon changed as world harvests improved and surpluses of grain and other commodities developed. The price of the products rose but by less than the costs of inputs and it was not possible to continue to compensate with even higher yields and greater efficiency.

Farms in the UK certainly benefited from membership of the EEC and the strong farm lobbies in Germany and France. Price cuts were not so severe as they might have been had Britain been outside Europe. The fall in farm incomes was not equal: arable farmers, certainly the larger ones, continued to get a good income, but live-stock and grassland farmers fared much worse, thus illustrating the old saying, 'Up corn, down horn'.

MECHANISATION AND TECHNOLOGY

Farm mechanisation and a reduction in labour continued, with much argument as to whether machinery was driving labour off the land. Rising wages tended to encourage the introduction of machinery but a much more positive influence was the use of machines to reduce, or even eliminate, grinding hard work. Sugar beet and potatoes are today handled almost entirely by machinery which has replaced hand work. Machines have the capacity to handle large areas of crops, making them attractive to large farms or contractors. Farms,

A tractor and six-furrow plough

especially those producing arable crops, have got steadily larger; one man, with a suitable tractor and plough, can cover up to 8 hectares (20 acres) in a day, but this equipment needs to be used to capacity if it is to repay the capital costs. It is unlikely that we shall ever see a return to labour-intensive farming systems, as mechanisation is here to stay. Old-style farming may look romantic but was hard on men and horses. Would anyone wish to undertake it again?

The development of a successful milking machine and dairy system allowed one man to milk up to 100 cows so that large dairy herds became the norm, even on family farms. Livestock mechanisation is more difficult than arable but automatic feeding systems have enabled a small labour force to take care of and manage large numbers of pigs and poultry. Sheep and beef cattle are still managed extensively, although even here hill shepherds use four-wheeled drive vehicles or trail bikes to get round larger and larger flocks. With falling prices and pressure towards even larger sheep flocks in the UK, we may well see the 'minimal care' which has long been established in New Zealand and Australia.

Rapidly increasing production in the 1980s and the build-up of stocks of butter and skimmed milk powder led to the introduction of

EEC dairy quotas in 1984. It was no longer possible to meet falling margins by raising output, either by keeping more cows or by increasing yields per cow. Herds were reduced in size and a greater emphasis placed on production of milk from home-produced feed, such as grass and grass silage, with a reduction in feeding purchased concentrates. More silage sometimes led to more silage effluent with consequent dangers of polluting water courses. More intensive grassland utilisation, using greater quantities of nitrogen, increased the possibility of its leakage into water supplies. These effects were not welcomed by those concerned about the environment.

After the introduction of quotas for milk production, attempts to reduce arable output, especially cereals, saw new measures like co-responsibility levies and stabilisers and set-aside, which removed land from cropping on either a long term or rotational basis. Farmers have also been encouraged to diversify, that is to move into other land-based activities like pony-trekking and tourism, and to add value to produce, such as making speciality cheeses.

There is also much interest in the possibility of using set-aside land to grow fuel crops – short term, like miscanthus, or more permanently from willow or poplar. The methods of production have been worked out but large-scale outlets are not yet available and fuel crops cannot compete with fossil fuels at present prices. Some EC countries are actively encouraging the production of 'bio-diesel' based on rape oil from their own farms.

ENVIRONMENTAL IMPACTS

In the late 1960s a few farmers, advisers and others interested in the environment began to express concern about the effects of intensive, high-technology farming on the countryside and its wildlife. Encouraged by government grants designed to remove 'obstacles to cultivation', some farmers, especially in the arable east, embarked on extensive hedgerow removal. This was done not so much to gain extra land, as to reduce the labour of hedge trimming and remove a perceived source of arable weeds. Although many of the hedges dated mainly from the last enclosure movement, this return to the open fields of the 18th and early 19th centuries was not welcomed by the public.

The use of organochlorine insecticides which persisted in the food chain had disastrous and unforeseen effects on raptors which failed to breed. There was a sharp decline in the numbers of kestrels, sparrow hawks, peregrine falcons and even golden eagles. When the

Spreading slurry on frozen ground is no longer allowed

full effects were understood these substances were phased out to be replaced with less persistent materials. Straw-burning, seen by farmers as an economic and hygienic method of disposing of a waste product, also attracted public attention and was finally banned after the 1992 harvest. Alternative methods of disposing of surplus straw have had to be devised.

Farm practices can have other unforeseen and unwanted effects. The Game Conservancy Trust has shown that the absence of certain 'weed' plants in cereal fields reduces the number of insects living on those plants which are essential food for partridge chicks. Changes in farming practice can greatly improve the situation without reducing the crop yields.

In addition to these specific examples of the impact of farming on the landscape and the environment, a more general concern about the countryside, its appearance and the wildlife habitat has led to pressure on farmers to become 'environmentally friendly' in all their actions. Many government schemes have also been introduced to encourage activities such as tree planting, pond construction, wild flower meadows and the like on farms. Broader areas of countryside are covered by such schemes as Environmentally Sensitive Areas,

Farm Woodland Schemes and Nitrate Sensitive Areas, etc.

In 1969 farmers and conservation interests first met together to consider how farming and wildlife and landscape conservation might be integrated – the Silsoe Conference. Out of this arose the Farming and Wildlife Advisory Groups, county-based groups bringing farmers and conservation interests together locally, many with a full-time Farm Conservation Adviser able to help individuals with practical, on farm, conservation advice.

The Agriculture Act of 1986 required the Minister of Agriculture, Fisheries and Food to consider aspects of conservation and public enjoyment of the countryside in addition to food production. Grants are now given for conservation under a multiplicity of schemes and in some cases, these can be a major part of farm income.

FARM STRUCTURE

Increasing farm size, the decline in the number of farm workers and a steady movement of urban-based people to the countryside have all had their effect on the rural scene and the rural economy. In 1993 there were 547,000 persons engaged in agricultural production, 2.1%

Modern arable landscape

of the total employed work-force. Of these 284,000 were farmers, 110,000 regular full-time workers and 146,000 part-time or casual workers. Productivity has risen: measured in terms of gross product at constant 1985 prices per man equivalent, it rose by 54% between 1980 and 1991. It is not surprising that the countryside looks so empty, because the work is done, rapidly and effectively, by very few people. Villages which once housed mainly farm workers or those in ancillary trades now contain few, if any, who work on the land; the majority of workers commute to towns each day. In more remote and attractive areas such villages may now consist mainly of holiday homes and so be even less viable.

Where farming is carried out on a large scale, produce, whether grain, potatoes or milk, must be stored, often refrigerated or dried and collected or delivered to factories. This may involve large storage buildings and many regular movements of lorries and tractors. This often conflicts with the newcomer's concept of country life, raising problems for the individual farmer. Cattle and sheep are seen as belonging to fields and not welcomed when they have to be moved along country lanes and roads.

The smaller labour force on today's farms is highly skilled. It has to be able to undertake a wide range of work using expensive and complicated machinery, often under adverse weather conditions. Training on the job is important but the modern farm worker will also have been trained at a county college and will continue to maintain and improve his/her skills through Agricultural Training Board courses. Since 1986 anyone who uses pesticides must have attended courses designed to provide adequate instruction and guidance about their legal use and correct handling.

Agriculture uses 18,530,000 hectares of land, about 76.7% of the total land area. About 30% of this is arable (under crops); the greatest part, about 60%, is grassland, either improved or rough grazing. Based on constant 1985 prices, agriculture contributed £5874 million to the UK gross domestic product, or 1.3%. Although only 2.1% of the work force is employed in agriculture, another 2.8% is engaged in food and drink manufacturing and a further 3.7% in food retailing. So the food industry, from field to supermarket shelf, employs altogether some 8.6% of the workforce.

FOOD SUPPLIES

Food retailing has changed dramatically over the years, with the number of food retailing businesses and outlets falling, especially specialist retailers like butchers and fishmongers. In 1991 there were 62,009 food retailing businesses with 82,572 outlets (shops or super-markets). Of the 62,009 food retailing businesses 74 were large grocery businesses with 8309 outlets employing 522,000 people. These large grocery retailers (supermarkets) accounted for 78% of the retail trade total turnover of £48,718 million in 1991.

The UK farming industry produces, at present, about 58% of all our food. Some things like tea, coffee and bananas cannot be grown here; of what we can grow, 74% is produced on our own farms. Self-sufficiency varies between commodities: whereas we grow 129% of our wheat, allowing 29% to be exported, we produce only 53% of our own sugar, 69% of our bacon and ham and about 19% of our fresh fruit.

By comparison with other countries in the EC, farms in the UK are large, averaging 67 hectares compared with 16.8 in Germany and 28.6 hectares in France in 1992. What is even more significant is that, in the UK, 17% of the holdings are 100 hectares and over and occupy 66% of the agricultural land. 66% of the holdings are under 50 hectares but have only 16.5% of the land. Many of these small farms are part-time, the occupier having another occupation, often con-nected with the agricultural industry. It is the large holdings which make the major contribution to agricultural output so that 20% of the farms contribute 80% of the produce. 63% of the farmed land is owner/occupied and 37% rented, a considerable change from the beginning of the century when 80% was rented.

Since 1986 the area of land used for cereals has declined from 77% to 67% of the arable area. Whilst land sown to wheat fell by 12%, the area used for barley has fallen by 20% and there was a rise in oilseed rape production of nearly 30% between 1986 and 1990. Oilseed rape production has since declined by some 3% following changes in price support arrangements. Other crops show increases: peas for harvesting dry and field beans rose by 62%. The area of land used for vegetables and fruit has fallen but more land is now used for bulbs, flowers and hardy nursery stock.

LIVESTOCK TRENDS

The size of the national dairy herd continues to fall. A reduction in EC milk quotas resulted in a 15% fall in cow numbers between 1986 and 1993. Beef cows rose by 33% over the same time. There are now about 44,000 dairy farms with an average herd size of 68 cows.

In 1991 there were 90,700 holdings with sheep and an average flock size of 223. In January 1992 the market subsidy on lamb, based on a direct deficiency payment, came to an end and was replaced by a headage payment on ewes – the Ewe Premium Scheme. At the same time the clawback of the subsidy on lambs exported from the UK, which made lamb exports uncompetitive, ceased. Producers are now much more dependent on the market for returns on lamb sales.

The UK is the most important producer of sheep meat in the EC, accounting for 35% of the total production. Between 1991 and 1993, exports of lamb to the rest of Europe increased by 64%, and 44% of the total UK production of lamb is exported.

Taking the hard work out of farming

A sheep quota has now been introduced which will restrict the expansion of the UK sheep flock. The quota limits the subsidy (the ewe premium) to a maximum number of ewes per farm (500 in the lowlands, 1000 in the hills). Above that number the ewe premium is reduced by 50% up to a total number equivalent to the numbers on the holding in the reference year of 1991. The sheep farmer, like the dairy farmer, has to operate within the restrictions of a quota.

Pig production has moved towards larger units. It receives no EC support and profitability depends on the relationship between feed costs and the price the producer receives for the product. There were 11,800 holdings with breeding pigs in 1991 with an average herd size of 62; over 75% were in herds of 100 and over. 59% of the fattening pigs were in herds of 1,000 and over, although the average herd on the 11,800 fattening holdings was 370 pigs. In response to public

concern about confining breeding sows, there is a marked trend
towards keeping breeding herds outside, although this system is
really only suitable for lighter, free-draining soils and can be un-
pleasant for both pigs and workers in periods of bad weather.

The number of laying hens continues to decline and at 32.8 million
in 1993 was 14% less than in 1986. The average flock size is just
under 1,000 birds but 72% are in flocks of 20,000 and over. More
free-range eggs are being produced but the bulk still come from
laying batteries or barn systems.

Broiler production continues to increase to meet the steady
demand for poultry meat. This is large-scale production with only
1,800 holdings with an average flock size of 41,000 and 57% in flocks
of 100,000 and over.

POLICY INFLUENCES

The public perception of the farmer is of someone who grows a
number of crops – certainly wheat and barley, potatoes and possibly
turnips or swedes. He (or she) will milk a herd of 40 or 50 cows, keep
some sheep, have a few pigs in styes and some hens running about the
farmyard. Of course the yard and the farm house will be picturesque,
no mud, and the sun must be shining. The farmer, despite being
heavily subsidised, is always grumbling, especially about the weather.
This image may be acceptable, but that of the agribusiness man with
his large fields and intensive livestock is not. What is the reality?

The most obvious change is the move away from mixed farming,
with a little of everything, to specialisation. Today's farm, with a
few exceptions, is likely to concentrate on two or three enterprises,
or perhaps only one enterprise. This enables the farmer and his
employees to develop the special skills needed and to concentrate
their efforts on what the farm is best suited to produce. This is
particularly so with livestock when pig, poultry and dairying are
carried out as specialist enterprises rather than part of a mixed farming system.

Farming systems remain diverse but are still influenced by their
location, soil type and fertility and the local climate. The lighter soils
in lower rainfall areas grow most of the crops; the wetter, hilly and
perhaps more attractive parts grow grass and keep livestock. There
will, of course, be places in between with varying patterns of crops
and stock.

For many years farmers wrestled with the problems of the weather
and with pests and diseases of both crops and livestock. They had

few external controls, the main one for tenant farmers being their tenancy agreement which usually set down limits as to what land might be cropped and often specified the crop rotation. Produce was sold locally so shelf life was no problem. In order to control diseases in livestock, some of which could be spread to humans, governments introduced restrictions on livestock movement and health schemes which have virtually eliminated such diseases as tuberculosis and brucellosis in dairy cows. Hygiene in milk production and farm dairies has been improved and tightened so that, with home refrigeration, milk will keep for several days, even in summer. Few now remember when milk had to be scalded as soon as it was delivered in summer to prevent it from going sour.

There are many other ways in which farming is directly affected by external factors which influence the ways in which crops are produced and livestock maintained and cared for. The production of food is seen as the first part of the human food chain and, therefore, it is subjected to high standards of hygiene and quality control. This is, of course, very necessary and desirable but adds to production costs and demands high standards of management. When wheat was harvested in sheaves and stored in ricks until threshing, it was often infested with rats and mice; a modern grain store must be kept free from vermin and birds which requires high standards of construction and management. Standards of cleanliness in milking parlours must be of the very highest and maintained at all times of the year, however much mud there may be outside. What may be relatively easy to achieve in a factory may not be so readily attainable on a farm. Livestock still retain their normal habits!

So as with other industrial activities, farming is affected by decisions taken in London, Brussels or at GATT (General Agreement on Tariffs and Trade) talks. Although many policy decisions are now taken in Brussels, detailed regulations and controls are formulated and enforced by our own government. The Ministry of Agriculture, Fisheries and Food has many responsibilities, including animal health and welfare, control of production through quotas, grants and subsidies, licensing and advice. In an attempt to harmonise production methods within the EU, Brussels sets out a large number of objectives covering many aspects of farming, food production and food handling. These may be interpreted and enforced in different ways in the countries making up the EU but will most certainly affect individual farms. These regulations may be enforced by MAFF or by the local authorities. New hygiene regulations designed to improve abattoirs may be too expensive for some small establishments to undertake. If these close, leaving fewer and larger establishments

Decisions taken here affect all farmers

operating then, inevitably, livestock must travel further for slaughter and perhaps wait in lairages overnight. The welfare of animals will be adversely affected, something which was not necessarily foreseen by those concerned about abattoir hygiene and design.

The GATT will, when fully implemented, affect the future of all farms as it will no longer be possible for countries to support commodity prices. The GATT objective is to encourage international trade free from tariff and other restrictions. It is claimed that this will create more employment worldwide and help underdeveloped countries by making it easier for them to export. These exports are likely to be food or other agricultural produce so competing directly with UK and EU farmers. Farmers, like other businesses, will have to compete in a wider market and accept lower world prices for their produce. Without support, commodity prices are also likely to fluctuate and become much more unstable. Large production units will be in a much stronger position to meet these new challenges than small family farms.

The capital cost of specialised machinery to handle produce and regularly supply large quantities of high-quality produce is so great that it favours the large-scale producer and cooperative handling and marketing. Small-scale producers, unless they are supplying specialised niche markets, find it difficult or impossible to compete.

Increased demands for access to the countryside and pressure on farmers to be more environmentally friendly, together with restrictions on the use of fertilisers and pesticides and the need to avoid pollution – desirable though these may be – increase costs and may make working practices more difficult. By and large the farming community accept the need for these changes and has adapted well to them. But the countryside and the way it is managed and farmed will also change. If the population of the UK wants high-quality food regularly available, then unless special arrangements are made to preserve small farms, farms will continue to get larger and production of both crops and livestock will be rigidly controlled at all times.

Supplying access to the countryside

The purpose of this book is to look, in detail, at the UK farm enterprises and to show how they have developed and how they are carried out. Besides such factors as climate, soil type, weather, crop varieties, breeds of livestock and so on, each enterprise is also influenced by EU and UK government policies, hygiene and other regulations; all these aspects will be examined in relation to current and future developments.

CHAPTER TWO

Arable Farming

BACKGROUND AND POLICY

Contrary to popular belief, farming in the United Kingdom is not predominantly concerned with the production of arable crops. Agriculture occupies about 18.5 million hectares, 77% of the total land area, and of this, only 5 million hectares are used for crop production. Over 11 million hectares are in permanent grass or rough grazing. 707,000 hectares of agricultural land are woodland, an increase from 543,000 hectares in 1986; farmers are planting trees for shelter from the wind, to improve the appearance of the countryside and to provide cover for wild game.

Ideal arable land is level and easily worked, well drained and with a low summer rainfall, especially during the harvest months of August and September. Such land in the UK lies mainly in the eastern counties, although there are substantial areas in the south of England and in the east of Scotland. These 'traditional' arable areas are in the counties of Essex, Suffolk, Norfolk, Lincolnshire and east Yorkshire; Shropshire and Nottinghamshire in the Midlands; on the light limestone and chalk soils in Hampshire. Wiltshire and the Cotswolds grew more grass during the agricultural depression between the world wars but moved to extensive cereal production during and after the Second World War of 1939–45.

What factors have influenced the development of arable farming?

It has become commonplace for those writing about, or commenting on, UK agriculture to make comparisons with the position before the Second World War. There are a number of reasons for this. Wartime pressures brought about rapid and dramatic changes in the countryside and in the production of crops and stock which created a considerable improvement in the fortunes of the farming industry.

16

Home-produced food of all kinds was needed. To those not directly concerned with farming, such changes altered the 'soft', largely unkempt countryside they had grown up with to a harder, more technical landscape. Nostalgia for the past, not always shared by those who actually experienced the working and living conditions, tends to colour the views of many towards the present-day agricultural industry.

A traditional harvesting scene from the late 1930s (Courtesy of Rural History Centre, University of Reading)

Agricultural output in the 1930s was overall very little higher, and in the arable sector substantially lower, than in the mid 19th century. British agriculture was one of the least intensive in Europe, and its unprofitability led to the withdrawal of labour and capital and the deterioration of the essential infrastructure. In 1939 there were only 3,600,000 hectares of arable, about 40% less than in 1870 at the end of the 'High Farming' era, which was a period when farming prospered through adopting many improvements in crop and livestock production, and when science began to come to the aid of the farmer. The UK as a trading nation relied on being able to purchase 70% of its food from overseas. Foods difficult to transport over long distances, such as milk and potatoes, remained important but cereal production fell by 26% between 1880 and the 1930s.

The countryside in 1939 was not the product of centuries of gradual evolution but of a dramatic reversal of a progressive trend which reached its peak in the 1880s. During the depression after the 1880s, arable reverted to grass and much of the grassland to woodland, scrub and waste conducive to the support of a large wildlife population.

Despite the depression, some arable farmers not only survived but prospered. One notable example (there are others) is Clifford Nicholson in Lincolnshire who, starting in 1930 with 484 hectares, expanded his business, based mainly on growing potatoes, so that by 1939 he farmed 3936 hectares. Land was cheap, there were no restrictions on individual initiative and land values were not distorted by such impositions as set-aside.

The 1939–45 war brought about rapid changes. Some 400,000 hectares of unproductive grassland were ploughed for crops during the first winter of 1939/40 and the ploughing campaign continued in order to produce crops to replace imported food which was difficult or impossible to obtain.

The agricultural depression of the 1930s and the shortage of food during the Second World War – which continued even more severely into the early years of peace – coloured the political approach to farming after the war. The 1947 Agriculture Act set out clear objectives for the farming industry. Although livestock, especially dairy farming, also received encouragement, it was the arable sector which made considerable advances and had the greatest impact on the countryside.

The old saying 'Up corn, down horn' described the policy. Crops which were immediately available for human consumption were needed rather than livestock products which required animals to convert crops and grass to meat. Cereals, especially wheat, and potatoes were in demand. Wherever possible, mechanisation was introduced and fertilisers used, although these were rationed. The main thrust lay in increasing the area under arable crops rather than raising yields from a smaller area.

The stability provided by the 1947 Agriculture Act laid the foundations for the steady expansion of the industry. Capital was invested in machinery which enabled fewer workers to produce the crops with less physical effort and under greatly improved conditions. Tractor cabs, regarded at first as rather 'cissy', are now standard equipment providing not only protection from the weather but also a safety factor should the tractor overturn.

THE INFLUENCE OF TECHNOLOGY

It was the introduction of selective herbicides in the late 1940s and 1950s which began the breakthrough in raising crop yields. Before this farmers had relied on crop rotations and cultivations to control weeds. Different crops grown in a field in a fixed annual sequence provided the opportunity to control weeds by cultivating the soil at varying times of the year. Root crops, like turnips or potatoes, planted in rows, could be weeded throughout the growing season; successful weed control depended on much hard work and favourable weather. Few cereal crops were weed-free, as anyone who has stooked sheaves including thistles will remember! Weeds compete with the crop for moisture and nutrients; herbicides control the weeds and help towards higher yields. Weed seeds often contaminate the harvested crop and herbicides eliminate or reduce this problem. But, as with most advances, there is a down side. Some plants – weeds in the crop – provide food for wild animals and birds, which have undoubtedly suffered as a result of clean, weed-free crops. The decline in the grey partridge can be attributed to this factor. Other species such as corn buntings and sky larks have also been affected.

Following the introduction of herbicides, a better understanding of the fertiliser requirements of the major crops, together with the introduction of improved crop varieties, led to further increases in yields. In the years after the Second World War a farmer might expect to harvest 2.5 tonnes of wheat from a hectare; today he would be disappointed not to achieve 7 tonnes from the same land.

There is no evidence that the underlying average increase in wheat yield is declining and most sources would forecast that it will continue to rise. Nitrogen fertilisers, which are an essential influence on yield, show little sign of any further increase in use; in fact for the last decade the use of nitrogen has remained constant, after a rapid increase in the previous 10 years. Any reduction in the use of nitrogen to much below present-day levels would certainly lower yields and increase the costs of production per tonne of wheat. It would also be impossible to attain the protein content of the grain needed for bread making.

The control of pests and diseases by chemical means also influences yield and is now near to maximum effectiveness. There is

Application of herbicide to control weeds

very little scope for increasing yields by this means and the future emphasis will need to be on the cost effectiveness and minimal environmental impact of chemicals rather than on their ability to increase yields.

In the past, at least half the increased yield of cereals, especially wheat, was through improvements and changes in agronomy – timely cultivations and weed, disease and pest control. Future advances in yield seem more likely to depend on plant breeding with the plants contributing more nutrients to the grain rather than the straw. Modern varieties are short-strawed and so less likely to lodge in bad weather. Cereal breeding programmes also place emphasis on in-bred disease and pest resistance.

Increased crop yields have thus been a major feature of arable farming in the past 30 years or so, more spectacular in the cereals, especially wheat, but also important with other crops such as potatoes and sugar beet.

In 1992 cereals accounted for 20% of the farmed land and were worth £2229M, nearly 15.5% of the total agricultural output. Horticultural crops, which occupied only 1.1% of the land, contributed 12.6% or £1817M to the total output and occupied fourth place. Milk was the leader at £2930M and 20.4%.

Another factor influencing the development of arable farming has been the introduction of winter-hardy varieties of cereals. Most wheat has been sown in autumn but barley was traditionally a spring-sown crop. Autumn-sown varieties of wheat and barley give higher yields than from crops sown in spring, but the swing to such varieties has created a concentration of work in the autumn. Land has to be cultivated and planted during a short period before the winter rains make the soils unworkable. The seasonal pattern of work has changed and so has the appearance of the countryside. There are fewer stubbles left over winter and so less is available for birds and animals to feed on during the winter.

Given such higher yields, coupled with guaranteed prices, intervention storage and favourable climate, it is not surprising that wheat production in the EC as a whole now exceeds internal demand. In 1988 the EC was 123% self-sufficient in wheat, but this average covers a wide range from France which was 249% self-sufficient, and had a surplus to export within the community or outside, to Portugal, which was only 35% self-sufficient. In that year the UK was 102% self-sufficient in wheat and had a small surplus to requirement. Wheat surplus to EC requirements can be taken into intervention stores, provided it satisfies the high quality standards, or exported. It is these exports which attract subsidies that influence world markets and have been the subject of so much discussion under the international GATT talks. It is interesting to note that, of a world production of 500 million tonnes of wheat, only 85 million tonnes, or 17%, is traded internationally.

In the UK only 20 to 30% of the total wheat planted is sown to varieties with bread-making quality, whereas in France and Germany 70 to 80% of the wheats grown are bread-making varieties. This reflects the maritime climate of the UK which is more suited to the production of high-yielding wheats with low protein content. The proportion of bread-quality wheats grown in the UK may increase through recent changes in EC policy on Intervention Standards. In future, wheats may only be accepted into intervention storage if they pass high-quality bread-making and other tests. Most UK traditional biscuit and animal feed wheats will fail the upper level of the quality test.

Farmers are reluctant to grow bread-wheat varieties because of their poor yielding ability compared to feed and biscuit wheats. Plant breeders are seeking to produce varieties which combine bread-making quality with higher yields, and some promising varieties are under test.

A crop which has made a strong impact (especially visually) on the British countryside in recent years is oilseed rape, its vivid yellow flowers being described by some as 'alien'. It was grown in eastern counties in the last century to provide colza oil for lamps, but production declined with supplies coming from Canada, where it is an important crop. In an attempt to reduce imports of vegetable oils in the 1970s, the EC introduced large subsidies for oilseed crops, including oilseed rape. Modern varieties produce an edible oil which can be used for cooking, as a salad oil or for making margarine. It is a combinable crop, needing no specialised equipment, and provides a useful rotational break from cereals. Not surprisingly the attractive subsidised price encouraged UK farmers to grow more of it and the crop expanded from nearly 300,000 hectares in 1986 to 445,000 hectares in 1991. Its popularity has declined more recently to 377,000 hectares as the price offered for the seed has fallen. Total UK production in 1988 was 947,000 tonnes out of a total for the EC of close on 5 million tonnes.

Sunflowers are a popular oilseed crop in continental Europe, but so far are only grown to a limited extent in the UK. Linseed, which was grown successfully just after the Second World War, has made a come-back (also encouraged by the EC Common Agricultural Policy) and its blue flowers may be seen as an interesting contrast to those of oilseed rape.

Horticultural crops, often grown under contract for freezing or canning, are becoming more important. Peas for the freezing industry have been grown for 30 years as have broad beans and other vegetables. Fresh vegetables grown to very exact specifications for supermarket chains are also of increasing importance, especially on larger arable farms. Although the area under vegetables declined from 140,000 hectares in 1986 to 136,000 hectares in 1991, the value of the produce rose from £807M to £1030M. The country is, however, still only about 80% self-sufficient and relies on imports for many vegetables that could be grown here. Some are grown out of season in other parts of the world to maintain supplies in the shops.

The arable sector of the agricultural industry has developed in response to changes in production methods and the demands of the market, either direct or as set out by government price support.

On the production side, mechanisation has reduced the numbers of workers required, as modern machinery can prepare land for planting very quickly. This is illustrated by the case study in Chapter 7. Sowing and harvesting are also high-speed operations, so reducing the adverse effects of weather. When there is a 'weather window', work can proceed rapidly and the produce can be stored safely under appropriate cover. Adequate storage, together with driers, chillers and conditioners, has been devised to aid the production of high-quality produce.

LEGISLATION

Some concern has been expressed about the extensive use of chemicals in crop production, and it has even been suggested that they are unnecessary. These include herbicides to control weeds, pesticides to control insects which may cause damage or loss of crop and fungicides to control fungal disease and which may be applied as seed dressings or to the growing crop. They protect the growing crop from damage and loss of yield. Treatments also contribute to the value of the product and ensure its safety and keeping qualities. Some weed seeds may be poisonous, as are the toxins produced by some diseases. Farmers and growers faced with the need to control their costs of production will certainly not use expensive materials unless they are necessary to protect the crop from pests and diseases which will certainly reduce yield and may very well render the crop unsaleable. High-quality, unblemished produce is demanded, whether for direct sale to the public – as fruit and vegetables – or as raw materials for food manufacturers.

Before a pesticide can be sold in the UK, a huge amount of data must be produced about its safety to the user, the consumer and the environment. Indeed, more than one-third of the £20 million cost of developing a typical new pesticide is taken up by safety testing. This data is scrutinised by the Advisory Committee on Pesticides, which must be satisfied that the product is safe. It is, of course, impossible to prove by experimental evidence that anything is absolutely safe, but pesticides used correctly present little dangers to users, consumers and the environment. It is interesting to note that much more is known about synthetically produced chemicals than about naturally occurring toxins which are often present in food.

All chemicals can be harmful under some conditions but not under others. Paracelsus, writing in the 15th century, said that, 'Everything is a poison, nothing is a poison, it is the dose that makes the poison.' Naturally produced food contains a wide range of toxins synthesised by plants to protect themselves from predators and pathogens. Few, if any, have been tested for human safety in the same way as pesticides.

Professor Bruce Ames of the University of California in the United States, speaking in London in 1992, said, 'Every plant is full of 50 or 100 chemicals that are natural pesticides that the plant uses to kill off insects. Cabbage is filled with isothiocyanates, these are natural pesticides in cabbage and in beans there are a different set of fifty.

What about cancer tests on these? They've only tested 70 or 80 of these natural pesticides, half of them came out positive, and the amounts are much more than anything synthetic. We calculated that you're eating 1500 mg a day of natural pesticides, but you're only eating 0.09 mg a day of synthetic pesticides; they're not even in the same league'.

The use of these agro-chemicals is carefully controlled and covered by several regulations which must be observed by the farmer and his employees. There should, for example, be no drift of a chemical spray during the application of pesticides and the spray operator must be fully trained and hold a certificate of competence in the safe use of pesticides.

Pesticides must be securely stored, kept dry and protected from frost, and stores must comply with the Health and Safety (HSE) regulations. Such stores may require planning permission and fire and water authorities should be consulted regarding location and construction. Fuel must also be safely stored. For example, diesel tanks should be surrounded by a bund which would hold the contents of the tanks if a leak were to occur.

Diesel storage to comply with current legislation

Sprayer operator wearing appropriate clothing (Farmers Weekly *and* CIBA)

The handling of pesticides on farms is covered by a number of regulations:

The Health and Safety at Work Act 1974 imposes general obligations on employers to ensure the health, safety and welfare at work of their employees; expects employees to take reasonable care of their own health, which includes wearing protective clothing; and requires suppliers to ensure that substances are safe and without risks to health when being used, stored, handled and transported.

The Control of Pollution Act 1974, among other things, prohibits the dumping of pesticides or their containers in or near waterways, ditches or ponds.

The Control of Substances Hazardous to Health Regulations (COSHH) controls the risks at the work place arising from substances which may be hazardous to health, it includes pesticides used by farmers and growers.

The Food and Environment Protection Act 1985 and *The Control of Pesticide Regulations 1986* are designed to ensure that pesticides are handled with care.

So far as humanly possible, these materials are tested, regulated and used responsibly. Pesticides will continue to be used, but in declining amounts. Those in current use will be gradually replaced by new materials which can be targeted for specific use so that less of the active ingredient is applied overall. The current average use of pesticides in the UK is about 5 kg of active ingredient per hectare and is declining; some 70% of our land never receives a pesticide treatment, so it is quite wrong to talk of the countryside 'soaked' in pesticides. It is noteworthy that by the year 2000 there will be about 0.5 hectares of land per person in the world, of which about half will be available for food production. Much land is poor-quality grassland and land is also needed for recreation, urban development and other uses. The area per person of land for food production can only become smaller, and intensive production will, therefore, continue to be necessary. Despite the current use of pesticides, the Food and Agriculture Organisation (FAO) estimate that 20–40% of the world food production potential is lost annually. Without the use of pesticides there would be massive food shortages. Nearer home, scientists at Rothamsted Experimental Station have estimated that if pesticides were banned in the UK, agricultural production would fall by 36% in the first year and by 48% after three years.

Much research effort and time have been, and still are being, spent on seeking alternatives to pesticides. Biological control is attractive and is increasingly being used on glasshouse crops which are grown in a controlled environment. Alternatives for arable crops grown in the open are, to date, minimal. Varieties resistant to pests and diseases are available, but their commercial life is often limited through the ability of the pest or disease to develop new races or strains. Yellow rust is a well-known example of this, as breeders of resistant wheat varieties appear to keep only a year or two ahead of new strains of the disease.

Genetic engineering can no doubt help with disease and pest resistance, but it may be difficult, if not impossible, to incorporate resistance to all important pests and diseases into one plant variety without affecting quality and yield. Perhaps the biggest area of public concern, after the actual use of pesticides, is that of chemical residues. Residues are by many assumed to be always present, although this is, in fact, rarely the case. MAFF carries out regular monitoring of fruit and vegetables, and in 1986 99% of home-produced crops and 98% of imported commodities were found to contain no detectable residues. Monitoring in Europe and other countries has produced similar results. The presence of residues is, in itself, of no importance; the toxicological impact must also be considered. If pesticide residues occur at all, they are nearly always below one part per million. The detection of residues is more a tribute to the sophistication of the analytical chemist than a tool in predicting a hazard to health.

Concern about pesticides and residues probably comes from public fear of increasing the risk of cancer. In the UK, pesticides cannot, in fact, be marketed if there is any risk that they might cause cancer. Tests are carried out on animals and bacteria, and any pesticide with a greater chance than one in a million of causing cancer (roughly the natural risk) is not accepted. A one in a million chance of dying from cancer from such a source is apparently equivalent in risk to smoking three-quarters of a cigarette or travelling 60 miles by car!

Professor Ames has also pointed out the relationship between diet, cancer and the use of pesticides. He says that diet is probably even more important than smoking in the epidemiology of cancer and that the most important component of diet in protecting against cancer is fruit and vegetables. 'The price of fruit and vegetables is important – wealthy people can afford organically produced food, but poor people can't and they'll buy less if the price is high. I think pesticides lower your cancer rate. Farmers who use pesticides are not fools because they get better yields and the price comes down; so pesticides lower cancer rates because they make fruit and vegetables cheaper.'

WATER SUPPLIES

Residues of pesticides and amounts of nitrates in drinking water are also issues of public concern, and regulations designed to control these impose restrictions on arable farming operations.

The EC Drinking Water Directive sets a maximum admissible concentration of 0.1 micrograms per litre (0.1 parts per billion) for a single pesticide and 0.5 micrograms per litre for total pesticides, irrespective of the toxicity of the chemicals involved. (1 part per billion is equivalent to 2 or 3 grains of salt in a swimming pool.)

These limits allow concentrations of such substances as arsenic and cyanide 500 times those of any pesticide, including those which are totally benign. Careful monitoring of water quality is, of course essential, but the UK government finds the current limits for pesticides scientifically unsupportable and has requested the EC to review them.

Whether or not a pesticide gets into water supplies depends on the properties of the particular chemical, the amount applied and the hydrology of the area. The vast majority of water supplies in the UK do not contain any pesticide residues and where residues do occur they are so small as to create no hazard. In terms of nitrates in drinking water the 1980 Community Directive places a maximum permitted level of 50 mg per litre of nitrate. There are some occasions when this level may be exceeded for a time, although the bulk of water supplies are below this level.

Concern about nitrate intake from water falls into two main areas. Firstly, infant feeds made with water with more than 100 mg per litre of nitrate may involve the risk of 'blue baby' syndrome, especially if there is also bacterial contamination of the water. This problem is, in fact, very rare: there have been 14 cases since 1945 (only one of which was fatal) and none in recent years. Secondly, there is concern that nitrates may react with food components in the stomach to create carcinogens. There is no clear causative link between nitrate content of water and gastric cancer. In fact, those areas of the UK with the lowest incidence of stomach cancers are those with the highest nitrate levels in water.

In the UK there have been no cases of ill health which can be specifically linked with high nitrate levels in drinking water. Nevertheless, stringent EC directives are in force which reflect the concern of the public to have available pure and uncontaminated sources of food and water.

Nitrogen is, of course, an essential element of plant growth and, in the UK, it is the first limiting nutrient to yields in non-legume crops. Without fertiliser nitrogen, supplies of nitrogen from the soil restrict crop yields to between one-third and one-half of their full potential.

A viable agriculture depends on nitrogen fertiliser and the intensification of crop production correlates well with its increased use. Between 1950 and 1980 the amount of fertiliser nitrogen applied to winter wheat increased from 30 to 145 kg/ha and average yields rose from 2.5 to 5.75 t/ha. Other crops have responded similarly to fertiliser nitrogen and adequate supplies of other essential plant nutrients such as phosphate and potash.

Nitrate can be carried from the soil into water supplies and there is no doubt that nitrate levels in water in some aquifers and rivers have risen over the last few decades. Some supplies exceed the EC levels for nitrate and, to comply with the regulations, water undertakings have either had to remove the excess nitrate, which is an expensive process, or to blend water high in nitrates with supplies containing lower levels in order to produce bulk supplies meeting the standard. The cost to the UK of meeting the 50 mg/litre limit on nitrogen concentration has been estimated to be £199M over the next 20 years.

To be available to crops, nitrogen must be present either as nitrate or ammonia. Nitrate is soluble in water and so excess rain will leach or wash it out of the soil. Ammonia is held firmly on the surface of the soil particles but is converted to nitrate by soil bacteria. It makes no difference to the leaching whether the nitrate originates from chemical fertiliser, organic manure or reserves in the soil itself. Most nitrate leaches during the winter and the amount lost depends, therefore, on what is left in the soil after harvest. Winter wheat, for example, leaves very little of the fertiliser nitrogen applied in spring in the soil after harvest. Nearly all the applied nitrogen is either in the crop (and removed) or in the soil organic matter.

Bacterial action on soil organic matter produces a considerable amount of nitrate and this is the main source of nitrate leaching. Using nitrogen fertiliser in the autumn will, of course, add to the problem; farmers are aware of this and nitrogen is rarely applied to autumn-sown cereals.

Fertiliser trials have been carried out at Rothamsted Experimental Station on a range of crops for 150 years, some on Broadbalk Field which has been under continuous wheat for over 100 years. Between 1877 and 1884, soils that had been left bare and unmanured since 1870 leached 45 kg/ha of nitrate nitrogen a year. This is the same amount as is lost from soil carrying a fully fertilised wheat crop.

In another experiment some plots have received farmyard manure and others chemical manure for over 100 years. The farmyard manure plots contain more nitrate nitrogen which is vulnerable to leaching, than do the plots receiving chemical fertiliser.

Old permanent grassland releases vast amounts of nitrate when ploughed: one such site at Rothamsted lost 4000 kg/ha of nitrogen during the first 18 years after ploughing. During the Second World War and immediately afterwards, large areas of grassland (1 million acres in the winter of 1939/40) were ploughed. The resulting release of nitrate no doubt made a major contribution to the nitrate now appearing in water supplies, especially the aquifers under chalk and limestone soils.

High speed seed-bed preparation

The conclusion from all the published data is that the nitrate that leaches from arable land comes mainly from the breakdown of soil organic matter and crop residues. Very little comes directly from unused fertiliser if applied at the recommended rates. Fertiliser use therefore cannot be blamed for all nitrate pollution; nevertheless, public fears about adverse health effects have persuaded politicians to restrict nitrates in drinking water, although as discussed above there is no conclusive evidence that they are harmful.

Some leaching of nitrates cannot be avoided – rivers contained nitrates long before farming began. It is sensible to try to reduce nitrate leaching as much as possible but, as the experimental evidence shows, it cannot be eliminated. Even the drainage from bare land contains substantial amounts of nitrate.

There are two basic approaches to limiting the loss of nitrates from soils overlying aquifers: using less fertiliser nitrogen and 'nitrate trappings' (growing a crop in the field to trap the nitrogen during the winter).

The government introduced a Pilot Nitrate Scheme in 1988 to test the effectiveness of specific changes in agricultural practice. In 1990 the Scheme incorporated ten Nitrate Sensitive Areas (NSAs) covering sandstone, chalk and limestone groundwater sources with high or rising nitrate levels. Within these designated areas farmers face restrictions on the crops they grow, their farming methods and the use of fertilisers. For adopting these changes to their agricultural practices they receive financial compensation. There are also nine Nitrate Advisory Areas where farmers receive advice about methods to reduce nitrate leaching but are not obliged to adopt changes. They do not receive compensation.

As part of the agricultural and environmental package, another 22 voluntary Nitrate Sensitive Areas will be set up where farmers receive cash incentives if they comply with rules designed to cut the leakage of nitrates into water supplies. Some of these are areas with light, easy-to-work land on which potatoes are grown. The NSA rules have been modified to allow potatoes to continue to be grown.

Seventy-two Nitrate Vulnerable Zones (NVZs), covering 650,000 ha, have been designated in England and Wales, mainly in East Anglia and the north of England, with one in Clwyd. In these zones farmers face tight restrictions on the amount of fertiliser and manure they can apply to the land, coupled with controls on their farming activities. The controls range from banning the spreading of manure when snow is on the ground and installing new facilities for manure storage, to keeping detailed records of farming operations and manure and fertiliser applications. Unlike farmers in the voluntary Nitrate Sensitive Area schemes, farmers in Nitrate Vulnerable Zones will receive no compensation for the restrictions placed on their operations.

All farmers, whether in designated areas or outside, are advised to follow the MAFF Codes of Good Practice for the Protection of Soil and for the Protection of Water.

ORGANIC FARMING

Organic farming and 'organic' produce are presently attracting much interest. This involves producing crops without chemical fertilisers and pesticides to recognised organic farming standards and registered with the United Kingdom Register of Organic Food Standards (UK-ROFS). However, the cost of such produce to the consumer is high because yields are lower and, in the case of fruit and vegetables, much produce may have to be graded out due to damage from pests.

Organic producers are usually supplying a niche market so that if production rises they find that market returns are often too low to maintain the system. Organic farming, as currently practised, would not be sustainable in the long run and would be unable to provide the volume of food required by the large and increasing world population. At present 0.3% of the arable land in the UK is farmed organically and only 1.14% of food sales are organic foods. Even if those organic enthusiasts who forecast a doubling of production were right, there would still be less than 1% of the arable land managed in this way.

To be successful, organic farming requires large inputs of organic manures either as farmyard manure or ploughed-in short-term grass leys. With the demand for livestock products tending to fall it is difficult to see, in the long term, where the supplies of organic manures are to come from to practise organic farming on a much larger scale than at present.

Organic systems carried out during the past were not always sustainable in terms of crop nutrient. The Norfolk Four Course rotation (wheat, roots, barley, ley) is often quoted as a good example, but calculations show that nitrogen, phosphate and potassium were 'lost' in the grain and from livestock sold off the farm. The introduction of superphosphate, patented in 1842, and potash salts in 1860 prevented a major decline in soil fertility. Feeding large quantities of imported oilseed cakes to cattle in yards also brought nutrients into the system.

Referring again to Rothamsted Experimental Station, experiments there have shown that crop yields from fertilisers and farmyard manure are closely comparable, which indicates that organic farming systems are not inherently more sustainable than good husbandry practice using inorganic fertilisers.

CONTROLLING PRODUCTION

One of the effects of the EC agricultural policy in the last twenty years has been the production of surpluses of several commodities. A system which removes supplies which are surplus to market demand into intervention storage, combined with rising levels of production through the application of new technology, encourages overproduction. The signals to the producers are distorted, leading to some unsuitable land continuing to produce crops, often at high costs in resources used and in effects on the environment.

Agricultural production and marketing have been 'managed' for many years in most countries. Governments need to ensure adequate food supplies and to avoid shortages. Market forces, although balancing production with demand in the long term, often tend to produce a cyclic effect with many agricultural commodities having fluctuating prices and supplies. Governments also wish to maintain a viable farming community, maintain the rural community and ensure that land is available to expand production in the event of an emergency.

On a macro scale, agricultural production is influenced most by the size of the area under crops. During the Second World War, for example, farm output was increased by ploughing grassland (often under statutory orders) for wheat and potatoes. Current attempts to control production therefore centre on methods to encourage farmers to reduce their area of arable land, rather than reducing yield per area of crop.

The system of set-aside, whereby the land stays idle, was first introduced in the United States nearly 50 years ago in order to reduce cereal production and to secure environmental benefits such as the control of soil erosion. In the mid 1980s it became increasingly clear that the EC would have to take similar measures to counteract the continuing increase of surpluses, and set-aside was introduced in 1988. At first this was voluntary; payments were offered to farmers who set-aside 20% of their arable land and did not grow crops on it for a period of 5 years. The scheme was not very successful in reducing cereal production, as the actual set-aside land was usually not the most productive. It was not very popular as payments for set-aside did not match the returns from average crops.

As part of the CAP reforms (1992), area payments will be made for certain arable crops. In order to claim these payments, farmers, except those with very small farms, must set-aside 15% of their arable land. Such land must be cared for so as to maintain good cropping conditions and must not be used for agricultural production of any sort (including grazing) but it can be used for certain non-food crops. Such set-aside land may be non-rotational or rotational. Under the rotational scheme land will only be eligible for set-aside once every six years, so farmers will have to rotate their set-aside land round the farm. Such land will, in some respects, be like an old-fashioned fallow. The main difference between rotational set-aside and a fallow is that the land must either carry a sown green crop or natural regeneration during the winter months and this must remain untouched until 1 May. This is to prevent nitrate leaching from what would otherwise be bare ground. After 1 May the cover may be 'destroyed' and the land ploughed. Non-rotational set-aside will involve a commitment of 5 to 6 years and a higher percentage than rotational and it aims to produce environmental benefits during this period.

There are other schemes, some attached to the set-aside arrangements, designed to enhance the environmental value of removing land from cultivation. These include a Farm Woodland Scheme to encourage farmers to plant trees, especially broadleaved in small areas; a Meadowland Scheme to encourage public access; and a Countryside Premium Scheme which provides extra payments designed to encourage the management of set-aside land to benefit wildlife and the landscape. The Countryside Premium Scheme is only available in seven selected counties.

THE FUTURE

It is very evident that in recent years arable farming has become much more complicated than selecting the crops and their varieties best suited to the farm, the chosen market, the land and judging the weather. Today's farmer must also juggle with regulations covering the use of chemical inputs, the possibility of nitrates leaching into water courses and aquifers and rules regarding how much of the farm may grow crops in any year. Set-aside may be 15% in 1993 but could be more or less in the future, depending on how the EC

A modern combine harvester cutting, threshing, chopping and spreading straw

assesses supplies of the main arable crops. So farmers need to learn how to handle change.

Whilst farms with less than 15.51 hectares of cereals may not be required to set-aside land, they must comply with regulations concerning safety, the use of chemicals, nitrate leaching, etc. Turnover is critical on all farms but much more so on a small unit where there is little, or much less, flexibility. The market is dominated by the large outlets that wish to source supplies in very large bulk to be assured of continuity and to have guarantees about methods of production. All these pressures will, inevitably, increase the move towards larger, highly mechanised units. Large farms have more flexibility of cropping, produce in bulk and can afford to employ, either directly or under contract, the necessary high levels of expertise needed to meet the exacting standards laid down by regulations and by supermarkets.

Farming continues to be both an art and a science – applied biology – but requires a high degree of professionalism in order to survive under current conditions. It is understandable that the public, through politicians and the media, should express concern about production systems and press for food which is wholesome and nutritious. However, there is a danger that pushing for very low limits or even the complete absence of some residues or restricting cropping systems so as to reduce nitrate leaching may make it impossible to grow certain crops on some of the most suitable soils. Such moves could well result in food being imported from countries perhaps less concerned or less able to enforce regulations. It would be ridiculous to make UK farming so difficult or even impossible that it would be necessary to rely on imports from farms over which we have no control at all. The answer must lie in a balanced approach, with farmers encouraged to meet the needs of fully tested research programmes.

CHAPTER THREE

Dairy Farming

INTRODUCTION

The dairy cow is the most important animal in the UK farming industry, as milk and dairy products currently represent some 20% of total farm output. Being a ruminant, it is able to convert grass, forage crops, arable by-products and a wide range of other feeds, including concentrates, into milk – a high-value, nutritious human food. The dairy cow is also an important source of calves for the beef industry (some 65% of beef cattle being bred from dairy cows), and dairy cows at the end of productive life provide a major raw material for the manufacturing sector of the meat industry.

The milk now produced on UK dairy farms is some of the highest quality in Europe or even in the world. Improvements in animal health, breeding, feeding, machine milking and refrigeration have contributed to it being a safe and reliable product every day of the year. Almost half of the milk currently produced is consumed in liquid form, the remainder being manufactured into an ever-increasing range of dairy products from cheese and butter to ice-cream, yoghurt and liqueurs. High-quality milk with minimal unwanted bacterial content and absence of any trace of antibiotics is, of course, essential to the manufacturer of many of these products, which depend upon the growth of specific micro-organisms. The shelf-life of liquid milk is now claimed by many retailers to be over seven days due to the use of well-designed clean equipment, good hygiene techniques and, for most supplies, pasteurisation.

The provision of such high-quality milk and dairy products has not happened overnight but slowly and progressively (often accelerated in wartime) over the last hundred years. Before efficient train or road transport systems were established, much of the milk for the industrially based towns and cities in the 19th century was produced from herds actually housed within the urban areas. So-called 'flying' herds were operated, based on newly calved cows being transferred from outlying farms, usually milked three times per day for one lactation only and then sold for meat. It was apparently much easier to transport hay into town dairies and manure back to the country than to bring in milk which would soon go sour. Deliveries from these town dairies to the customers were twice a day, especially in the summer months, because of the poor keeping quality of the product and the unavailability of refrigeration. The health of the cows, as well as the people working with them, was often a cause for concern, operating as they did, in dark, badly ventilated underground cow-sheds. Tuberculosis, for example, spread rapidly from an infected animal. It was not until the Tuberculosis Order of 1925 and the Milk and Dairy Order of 1926 that legislation was enacted to improve health standards, and an Attested Herds Scheme was introduced in 1934. By 1960 the whole country was free from tuberculosis.

It is interesting to note the important contributions of particular innovators to developments in the agricultural industry. Arthur Hosier of Wiltshire is typical of the many splendid examples in the dairy industry. During the depression of the 1920s and 1930s many dairy farmers went bankrupt and had to leave their farms. Recognising a market for fresh milk, at an affordable price, in London, Hosier developed a system of extensive, low-cost forage-based production on the chalkland soils of the Wiltshire Downs. Inexpensive cattle

Hosier bail milking (Courtesy of Rural History Centre, University of Reading)

were imported from Ireland, grazing grass in the summer and outwintered with kale as a major source of forage. Hosier developed a mobile milking machine known as a bail with a vacuum pump powered by a tractor. Electric fences were used to control the herd, and the bail frequently moved onto 'clean' grass. The churns of milk were taken to the farmyard for effective cooling (using cold water) before delivery to the local station and subsequent transport on the Great Western Railway to London. Until a reliable business relationship could be established with the dairy companies that bought the milk, a farm employee had to travel on the train with the milk in order to collect the cash for the consignment.

The fact that the producers were such weak sellers and virtually exploited by the milk buyers led in 1933 to the establishment of the Milk Marketing Board, which has proved to be one of the most successful organisations for the marketing of any agricultural product in the country. It took the responsibility to collect the supplies from every milk producer, however isolated from the market, and to negotiate price, deliver, and collect the payment from the buyers. Producers then received a monthly milk cheque from the MMB from the 'pool' value of all milk produced.

Once such a reliable outlet for milk was established, diary farming soon became popular as a suitable enterprise for new entrants into farming. Many young people, often initially operating on a part-time basis, were able to use their limited capital resources to purchase dairy cows and, with the regular monthly income from milk, cover the cost of their expenses and at the same time accumulate funds to expand their herds. The introduction of EC milk quotas in 1984 effectively eliminated milk production as a suitable enterprise for new entrants with limited capital resources. Each dairy farm now has a restriction on the annual quantity of milk which can be produced, without risking a high financial penalty (a levy being charged if the national quota level is exceeded). Quota can be leased or purchased by one producer from another but as the amount marketed is small, prices are too high to be justified by a new producer with minimal capital. The cost of buying a dairy cow is approximately £1000 but the cost of purchasing the quota to sell the 6000 litres that animal would produce annually would be at least £3000. Issues of government policy affecting dairy farmers will be discussed below.

With the objective of ensuring that milk for the consuming public is safe and reliable, a range of legislation has been established over the years, which affects not only the animals but the people and the facilities. Before a farmer can produce milk for sale (rather than for calf rearing or as a house cow), the premises must be registered with

MAFF under the Milk and Dairies (General) Regulations 1959. If there is a change of occupier of the holding, a new licence has to be obtained. The regulations require the buildings in which the cows are milked to be located and constructed so that there is no risk of contamination of the milk. A milking parlour, for example, should not be close to a manure store, and if feed is stored above the parlour, dustproofing is required. Adequate light and ventilation have to be provided and dung and mud not allowed to accumulate. A separate milk room is required for the bulk storage tank. There must be a suitable and sufficient water supply for equipment cleaning, as well as for animals to drink. If a person engaged on a farm is aware that he or she is suffering from a notifiable disease, the Medical Officer of Health of the district has to be notified.

LOCATION

As grass, in the grazed or conserved form, is the major component of the cow's diet, a greater proportion of the dairy herds are to be found in the higher rainfall areas of the north, west and south-west of the country where grass grows most reliably. Few dairy herds operate in hill and upland areas due to the problems of making silage and hay in the often difficult terrain. Milk collection would also be a problem, especially in the winter months, as all supplies are now collected by bulk tankers. Some herds are, of course, located in the drier regions of the south and east, often on holdings which have a range of arable crops. In these situations, the diet of the cattle, therefore, often includes components like reject potatoes, misshapen carrots and brussel sprout stalks, as well as home produced cereals. The farms usually have an abundant supply of straw from a cereal enterprise so that winter accommodation commonly involves loose-housing on a deep straw bed, and the resultant farm yard manure is a valuable input to the arable rotation. Cereals are rarely grown on dairy farms located in the higher rainfall areas; straw for bedding is, therefore, more expensive and cubicle housing systems have been developed, with manure-handling based on slurry (a semi-solid mixture of dung and urine).

ENVIRONMENT

The need for all livestock farmers, but particularly dairy farmers, to be aware of the impact of their operation on the natural environment has been particularly highlighted in recent years. There has been an accumulation of legislation, codes of practice and guidelines which have reviewed the whole area of pollution control. The Water Act 1989, for example, established the National Rivers Authority (NRA), which is responsible for environmental protection and pollution control. The Control of Pollution Regulations 1991 have a major impact on the design and construction of new facilities for the storage of slurry (as well as silage and fuel oil). Although existing facilities are currently exempt from the regulations, the National Rivers Authority can serve notice on a farmer to improve the facilities if they are considered to be a significant pollution risk. Some grant aid is currently available for such improvements but a number of producers faced with the need to meet the requirements of this particular legislation will not be in a position to justify (or even obtain) the capital sums needed for the purpose. Tenant farmers are often in an even more serious situation than owner-occupiers. Unless their landlord is prepared to contribute to such costs, or agrees to appropriate compensation should the tenancy end, a number will be forced to discontinue dairying or even farming in any form. The regulations are another factor influencing the economics of milk production and also therefore the continued increase in the size of dairy herds.

Registered milk producers and sales of milk, United Kingdom, 1955–6 to 1991–2

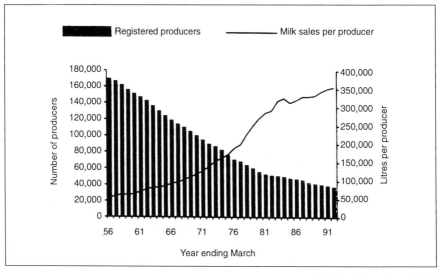

(Milk Marketing Board 1993)

HERD SIZE

The average size of herd has continued to increase over the years and is now 68 cows. Even the imposition of quotas did not slow down the trend, as the larger, often more successful producers have been able to buy or lease quota from the others.

The graph on page 40 demonstrates the marked reduction in the number of producers whilst at the same time the level of milk sales per producer has increased.

Other influences on herd size include resource availability, especially capital and labour, general layout of the farm such as access to grazing and building type. Traditional stone buildings where the cattle are housed, milked and fed in cowsheds or byres, as for example to be found in the Yorkshire Dales and in parts of Wales, are more difficult to expand than straw yards or cubicle sheds. A number of large herds have been established in recent years, and in fact 10% of all dairy cows are now in herds of over 200. Although milked in one parlour, the cows in such herds are normally subdivided into groups for housing and feeding according to month of calving, yield level or perhaps age (first-lactation heifers are frequently kept in a separate group). This minimises any bullying and provides a much-reduced level of stress on the animals.

Whilst herd size has been increasing over the years, so has individual cow yield. In the 1940s it was only 3000 litres per cow per year whereas the average yield is currently 5300 litres. Genetic variation within herds results in a wide spread of yield with some cows now producing over 10,000 litres per year. There are in fact a few herds with the herd average now over 10,000 litres.

BREEDS

Since the Second World War, when Shorthorns and Ayrshires were particularly popular breeds, the number of black and white animals has markedly increased to the current point at which they represent over 90% of the national herd. Until the 1970s, most black and white cattle were Friesians, either British or with some Dutch influence. Since then, however, a notable feature of UK farming has been the increasing influence of the Holstein breed. Most of the 'new genetics' originated as semen, embryos or imported stock from North America – in the earlier years from Canada but more recently from the USA. The cows of this breed are of a more extreme dairy

A herd of Holstein Friesian cows awaiting milking

type as they tend to be larger, produce higher yields and have better udder conformation than the British Friesian, although the bull calves are less valuable for beef production.

Although the Channel Island breeds – Jersey and Guernsey – are small in number (together only 4%) they have established a significant place in the 'market' particularly for 'breakfast milk' because of its higher milk fat and protein levels, as well as colour. Shorthorns, are still milked in a few herds and Ayrshire have maintained their place on many farms, particularly in their home region of Scotland, where they still make up 10% of the herds.

Although hybrid animals are in widespread use in the poultry, pig, sheep and beef sectors of the industry, it appears that it will be some years (if ever) before the typical dairy cow is other than a single breed.

BREEDING

As it is the birth of the calf that 'triggers' milk production, it is therefore important for the cow to become pregnant again during lactation and ideally produce the next calf one year after the previous one. The ideal lactation is 305 days with 60 days dry (not producing milk) prior to the next calving. It has been estimated that for every day over 365 between calvings, the dairy farmer loses £3 in 'lost' milk and calf value. As the gestation period averages 281 days, the cow needs to conceive some 84 days after calving if she is to produce the next calf one year later. The average length of productive life of a dairy cow is between four and five lactations, although this varies from one or two to over ten. To maintain or increase herd size, it is usual for newly calved heifers, either home-bred or purchased from other farms, to join the herd. To obtain suitable calves for future replacements, the 'better' cows in the herd are bred to bulls of the same breed. Since the 1950s artificial insemination (AI) has increasingly replaced natural service. Although initially questioned by some observers as 'interfering with nature', it has proved to be a safe, reliable and economic method of cattle breeding, as well as minimising the danger from having to handle temperamental bulls on commercial farms. At that time, there was considerable venerial disease in the national herd which was effectively halted by the adoption of AI. Semen (stored at low temperatures in liquid nitrogen) from sires of outstanding merit can be used widely throughout the country and even internationally.

Embryo transfer (ET) technology has also been developed in recent years to the stage where, although not as yet economic in commercial milk production, it is widely used with pedigree stock to increase the availability of animals with particularly high genetic potential. In-vivo techniques were first developed involving insemination of the donor cow followed by 'flushing out' of fertilised ova at a few days of age and subsequent implanting in a surrogate mother. In-vitro techniques are now being developed by which ova recovered from live animals, or after slaughter in the abattoir, are fertilised in the laboratory and the embryo is then implanted in the surrogate. Further developments in this field will no doubt lead to the availability, as and when required, of twin calves and even to determination of the sex of the calf. This latter possibility although now available but as yet very expensive, would lead to a major increase in the efficiency of both milk and beef production enterprises. Female calves would then be obtained from a smaller proportion of the herd and from the better cows, leaving a higher proportion of the herd to produce high-meat-potential male calves by a beef sire.

As with AI in the early years, there is currently some concern as to the ethics of using this type of technology in animal production. With appropriate veterinary supervision and development of suitable codes of conduct, there should be every confidence that such practices will be of considerable benefit to mankind whilst causing no problems to the animals involved. In the future farmers and their stockpeople may have to confirm their competence in managing animals by undertaking practical and written tests. This procedure would no doubt be of considerable value in assuring the public of the use of ET and such techniques in animal breeding.

HEIFER REPLACEMENTS

Although some dairy farmers purchase their replacement heifers from the market or from specialist rearers, most rear their own. Research work as well as commercial experience shows that the heifers which calve for the first time at approximately 24 months of age become the most efficient dairy cows.

A suitable system of rearing involves suckling of the mother for the first day to obtain the first milk (called colostrum) followed by bucket feeding of whole milk for several days before transfer to reconstituted (lower cost) powdered milk until weaning at six weeks of age.

A number of husbandry tasks need to be undertaken by trained and skilled staff prior to weaning. Removal of supernumerary teats (over the required four) with surgical scissors and horn bud removal – as will be described in Chapter 4 in respect of calf rearing for beef.

Calves over 6 months of age can satisfactorily graze at pasture in the summer months, although supplementary concentrate feeding may be required to maintain a satisfactory growth rate. Vaccination prior to turn-out to prevent lungworm infestation is the norm as is the use of anthelmintic drugs during the grazing season to control intestinal parasites.

If a cow is to calve at 24 months, conception needs to take place at 15 months. Natural service with a bull such as an Aberdeen Angus which should produce small calves and avoid difficult calvings is the norm. The ideal weight of a Holstein/Friesian after calving is 500 kg, which can be obtained by an average growth rate of 0.7 kg per day during the rearing period.

FEEDING

Providing the cow with an optimum and economical ration at each stage of the productive year is a considerable challenge to the dairy farmer. When grazing at pasture in the spring and summer months, lactating cows can obtain all or most of their nutrient requirement from grass alone.

Nitrogen fertiliser applications to the pasture are necessary to maintain forage quality and quantity. Providing soil temperature has begun to rise before the first spring application is given and late autumn applications are avoided, a high proportion of the nitrogen applied will be utilised by the crop, so avoiding loss to the subsoil. In specific areas of the country (Nitrate Sensitive Areas) where water is abstracted for domestic drinking purposes, application of nitrogen fertiliser is restricted and compensation is provided to farmers. Less intensive livestock systems such as beef and sheep may be possible in such situations, but the need for regular reliable supplies of forage essential for efficient milk production rules out the dairy enterprise.

Winter feeding of dairy cows normally involves the use of a conserved forage such as hay or silage, although a few farmers grow specialised forages such as kale or fodder beet. Suitable weather conditions to make adequate quantities of high-quality hay are

Winter feeding

limited so that grass silage is the most common ingredient of winter diets. The process of silage making involves cutting and chopping the grass in the field with a forage harvester and then transporting it to a clamp or bunker in the farmyard, where it is packed and sealed, usually with plastic sheeting, held down by straw bales or old tyres. The material ferments by bacterial activity – conversion of sugar into acid in the anaerobic environment of the sealed clamp.

As with slurry mentioned above, silage effluent is potentially an extremely polluting agent because of its high biochemical oxygen demand (BOD). A few dairy farmers cut their grass at high-moisture content but have appropriate facilities to store the effluent (in this case, grass juice) for subsequent feeding to the animals. Most aim to reduce the moisture content of the grass by cutting during periods of dry weather and allowing the material to wilt before ensiling. In this way, effluent production can be reduced, if not eliminated. However, all silos are required to have appropriate drainage facilities to collect any effluent produced and this can be returned to the land in a diluted form. The practice of making silage clamps on bare soil is now discouraged, but thanks to the development of the technique for making baled silage, grass which cannot find a place in a silo can be adequately conserved, particularly if it is tightly wrapped in plastic. The baling machine (which can also be used to make straw bales on a cereal farm) picks up the previously cut and wilted grass, forming a large circular bundle of material.

In the warmer, drier areas of the country, particularly in the south, maize is becoming increasingly popular as a forage for making into silage for dairy cattle. As it is usually cut at a higher dry matter content than grass, effluent production is rare, and as maize is a crop which takes up considerable nutrients from the soil whilst growing, it is well suited to situations where slurry or farmyard manure has been applied.

Much debate has taken place, and some continues, regarding the possible use of bovine somatotrophin (BST) in milk production systems. This is a hormone that occurs naturally in the cow's bloodstream. Widespread trials in the UK and other parts of the world have shown that supplementation with this product, stimulates the cow's appetite so as to increase milk yields by 10–15%. Negligable side effects have been detected (slight increase in mastitis being reported from one trial in the USA). As injection is the current method of provision, many dairy farmers have stated that they will not use BST but the likely rejection of milk from treated cows by a sector of the market will no doubt influence their decision. One can imagine that it could have considerable benefits in specific situations.

Take, for example, a small herd whose production level is below quota as the end of the production year approaches. Without additional animals or extra labour, the cows can be stimulated to eat more and so help meet quota output. It is of interest to note that clearance has now been given for BST to be used in the USA. Unless strict labelling rules are introduced, it will be possible for UK consumers to eat imported US cheese made from milk produced by BST-treated cows without knowing it.

HOUSING

As mentioned above, a wide range of housing systems is used on dairy farms depending upon such factors as climate, straw availability and type of traditional building in the area. In many locations cattle can be outwintered, so saving on capital costs. There are problems, however: soil poaching, food wastage, diversion of nutrients from productive use to keeping the animal warm, as well as dirtier cows at milking time. For these reasons, as well as for the convenience of, for example, having light in a building enabling effective observation to be undertaken, most farmers choose to provide cattle housing. There are few farm jobs more frustrating than bringing (after finding) the herd from pasture for milking on a foggy morning!

As with other farm animals, MAFF has issued codes of recommendations for the welfare of cattle. These provide information on the design and operation of buildings and equipment to meet the health and behaviourial needs of the stock. For example, they provide stock with a dry lying area, ensure the absence of slippery floors, eliminate sharp edges to gates and fittings and allow for the segregation of sick animals. Recommendations also allow for a high standard of stockmanship. Trained and experienced people working with stock understand the needs of their animals – for comfort, appropriate diet, water, light, ventilation and exercise.

MILKING

This is an area of milk production which has seen considerable change in the last 50 years. Hand milking was replaced by machines on most farms by the 1950s. At that time milking was done in cowsheds, where the animals were also fed and housed. Because of the need to increase labour efficiency, specialised milking parlours

Milking in the 1940s (Courtesy of Rural History Centre, University of Reading)

were developed and installed on dairy farms, so that today, most cows are parlour milked.

The majority of parlours have a facility to provide concentrate feeding and increasingly such a facility is computer controlled, so allowing individual rationing of each cow. The main task of the milker is to prepare the udder by washing or dry-wiping before fitting the claw piece (or cluster). Automatic cluster removers (ACRs) have also been developed which take the cluster off the cow when milk flow has ceased. Electronic identification units can now be fitted to a neck collar on each cow which allows automatic feeding and milk recording, as well as possible diversion of unsuitable milk and perhaps, in the future, oestrus detection. With the increasingly stringent requirement to prevent any milk from cows being treated for mastitis infection with antibiotics getting into the bulk supply (as well as during the prescribed withdrawal period), an efficient animal marking system is required to pinpoint those cows whose milk should be discarded.

'Robotic milkers' which will also prepare the udder and fit the clusters automatically are under development. Although initially they are very expensive, one can visualise their considerable potential benefits on farms where the owner or stockperson could use their time to greater advantage in management and health checking than in the routine chore of milking.

Twice a day milking is currently the norm, with three times being practised in a few high-yielding herds, although robots will be programmed to milk four or even five times a day. Frequency of milking stimulates feed intake and hence milk production but one of the major advantages is to reduce the stress on the udder tissue and so lengthen productive life in the herd.

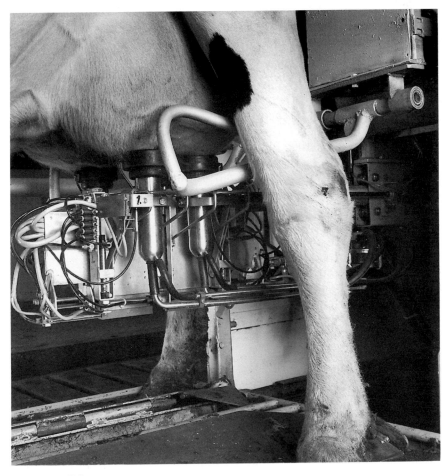

Robotic milking

HERD HEALTH

The dairy industry has a proud record of research and development programmes for the control of cattle disease, ensuring that milk is a healthy product for the consuming public. This involves the dairy farmer and his staff in being at all times observant and paying attention to detail in managing the cows, the housing and the equipment.

Mastitis is an inflammation of part or all of the udder caused by a bacterial infection. The bacteria enter the teat orifice from such sources as milking equipment, bedding or the milker's hands; the cow reacts by generating a migration of white blood cells into the udder to combat the infection. The number of these cells passing into the milk gives a measure of the level of sub-clinical mastitis (i.e. the infection does not show in the pre-milking sample taken by the milker). For many years the Milk Marketing Boards undertook a monthly count of these somatic cells from a sample taken from the bulk tank, so as to assist farmers in their health management. Now that payment for milk is also based on this measure, individual cow monitoring is being offered by the milk recording organisations as an aid to culling the individual animals which have extremely high cell counts.

Mastitis control is greatly assisted by a range of appropriate pharmaceutical products, particularly antibiotics. These are usually available from a veterinary surgeon prescription in tube or syringe form for infusion via the teat into the infected 'quarters' of the udder. As mentioned above, strict codes of conduct apply regarding disposal of milk from cattle under treatment, with severe penalties for supplies found to be contaminated. Each Marketing Board has a different penalty scheme; all pay a reduced price for a 'failed' consignment, and repeated failures can lead to licences being withdrawn. On some farms this milk is fed to calves, on others it is 'dumped' – but like silage effluent, it has an extemely high polluting potential because of its BOD and should certainly be kept out of water courses.

Brucellosis in cattle is a contagious disease which can cause abortion, in some cases infertility and therefore reduced milk yields. Since 1989 the UK has been designated as officially free of brucellosis (OBF). Biennial testing of all breeding animals over a year old is undertaken. Compensation is payable for animals which have to be slaughtered because of the infection.

Enzootic bovine leucosis (EBL) is a virus disease of cattle which causes changes in the blood and the development of tumours. It is present in a small number of imported animals and, to prevent spread, has been made a notifiable disease. A Cattle Health Scheme allows farmers to register as being free of EBL, so enabling them to be involved in intra-community trade in breeding cattle. Freedom from infectious bovine rhinotracheitis (IBR) can also be registered under the Cattle Health Scheme. This is another virus disease, usually affecting the nose and windpipe of the cattle. It can be controlled by vaccination, which in most cases is a justifiable expense.

Bovine spongiform encephalopathy (BSE), one of the latest cattle diseases to be identified, is causing as much concern to farmers and veterinary surgeons as to the consuming public. BSE has a long incubation period, measured in years, and there is no test for the presence of the disease in live animals. Symptoms normally start with a usually quiet cow becoming nervous, then aggressive – hence

A dairyman checking medicine stocks

the popular name, 'mad cow disease'. Lack of coordination of the hind legs when walking is the test used by veterinary surgeons to require slaughter. Early epidemiological studies indicated that all the infected cattle had been given feed containing ruminant protein as meat and bone meal – a practice undertaken for decades. The method of processing, however, changed over the years, and temperature regulations for sterilisation were altered. Sheep numbers increased, so that more by-product was included in animal feeds, so that cattle have most probably been exposed to scrapie (a disease of sheep similar to BSE) in their feed. In order to prevent any infection getting into the food chain, a ban has been placed on the availability of certain offal for human consumption.

There are other diseases which, although very serious when they occur, are rare; these include foot and mouth disease, anthrax and tuberculosis. Many farmers in the south-west of the country are concerned at the increase in tuberculosis, which has been associated with the increased number of badgers. Leptospirosis, which until recent years was also rare, is now an increasing concern as it affects people working with stock i.e. stockpersons and veterinary surgeons. Fortunately it can now be vaccinated against.

EUROPEAN UNION POLICIES AND QUOTAS

Dairy farming in the European Union (including the UK) has certainly not been free of troubles in recent years. Beset by surpluses and confronted by a world market in which EU supplies seriously depressed prices, politicians agreed in the 1980s that policy changes were required. Although cow numbers in the EU have fallen by 9% since 1970 and the number of herds has effectively halved, milk production is still increasing due to ongoing improvements in breeding, feeding and herd management.

In 1984, the cost to European taxpayers in supporting dairy farmers was increasing so much that drastic action had to be taken. Output control in the form of production quotas was imposed virtually overnight. Each country (and in some countries each dairy to which the milk from a number of farms was delivered) was allocated a specific level of quota. If in any year that quota level was exceeded, then the individual farms that were over their quota had to pay a levy or fine.

As the price of milk received by producers was based on the solids content, primarily on the butterfat and protein, there was a tendency for producers to raise the butterfat level of their output by dietary changes. This enabled them to increase their income within the fixed quota volume. This loophole was, however, closed in 1987, so that now when penalties are imposed for national over-quota production, the average butterfat content of the milk from individual farms is taken into account when calculating their level of excess production. It is therefore advantageous for producers to show an increasing interest in raising milk protein levels rather than butterfat output.

Reform of the CAP in 1993 extended the quota scheme to the year 2000. In the UK, deliveries to dairies in 1993 had fallen some 16% from the peak of production in 1983.

Since quota introduction, it has been legally possible in the UK to buy and sell quota but complications have arisen due to quotas being attached to land rather than to producers. A particular problem has been caused to farm tenants who have, for example at retirement, to agree with the landlord to a split in the value of the asset. The UK is also unique in the EU in having an annual leasing arrangement whereby producers likely to be over quota can lease for a season a quantity of quota from others who expect to fall short on production or who may even have sold their herd. Arrangements have to be completed and registered with the MMB by 31 December of the production year ending 31 March.

THE FUTURE

Milk production in the UK faces a number of challenges in the years ahead. Technical progress in breeding, feeding and cow management will no doubt be sustained so that the national quota level will be achieved by even fewer cows. This will not only have an effect on the calf supply to the beef industry, but also cause a further reduction in the number of producers. If further mechanisation and automation are to be introduced, average herd size will need to continue to increase to justify the capital investment required. Anxieties will perhaps continue in the context of food safety and in concern for optimum human diets in respect of medical advice on butterfat consumption.

After the planned departure of the statutory Marketing Boards due in November 1994, farmers will be free to sell their milk to any buyer. However, the growing concentration in the retail and wholesale sectors of the food industry should stimulate producers to cooperate as effectively as possible in order to negotiate with strength.

The need to prevent any negative impact of dairy farming on the environment will become even more important. Research and development will concentrate on ways to help farmers use slurry and effluent in a safe way, so avoiding pollution of watercourses.

Stockpeople will continue to be an important resource in dairying. Although as suggested, robots could well be introduced to take most of the chore out of milking, well-trained and motivated stockpeople will be even more essential. They will continue to check on health and assist with difficult calvings, and increasingly they will need to know how to deal with machine breakdowns – or know a man who can!

CHAPTER FOUR

Beef Cattle and Sheep

INTRODUCTION

Beef cattle and sheep have, over the years, fulfilled a major role in UK farming by converting grass and other forages into high-quality human food and supplying hides, skins and fibre which are valuable raw materials for manufacturing industry. Early man recognised the potential of these animals as providers of food as well as of clothing to protect him from cold, wet and heat. Today the range of products obtained from beef and sheep enterprises not only includes meat and offal, but also milk and other dairy products (from ewes), leather, wool (including astronaut's clothing), inputs for the pharmaceutical industry and the highest-quality medical suture tissue (from the skin of a steer's rump).

A small proportion of beef animals are reared in systems involving all-year housing. Many cattle and some sheep are housed during the winter months, but the majority depend predominantly for their nutrient supply upon grazing of upland pastures and permanent grass leys in arable rotations and forage crops such as turnips, swedes and kale. The intensity of grassland production with beef and sheep enterprises tends to be much lower than with dairy farming: less nitrogen fertiliser is used, clover is more often a component of the sward and there is minimal dependence on silage for winter feeding, especially with sheep. As housing systems for beef cattle are more commonly based on deep straw bedding than cubicles, slurry is not so commonly produced and these farms are less likely to cause water pollution problems than dairy farms.

As with other sectors of the farming industry, numerous technical and management developments have been introduced, leading in most situations to increased output in terms of land and labour use. Average size of enterprise has increased: the average beef herd carries 22 cattle and the average sheep flock is 225 ewes. Although there are farmers who specialise in either beef or sheep production, particularly in the hill and upland regions, a high proportion of beef cattle and sheep are found on farms which also have other enterprises like arable or milk production. The demand on these mixed farms for resources such as labour (for lambing) and buildings (for wintering) varies from one part of the year to another, so that with effective planning, it is possible to design and operate systems which successfully integrate crop and livestock enterprises to the financial benefit of the total farm business.

Production quotas for both beef and sheep were introduced as part of the CAP reforms in 1992. The objective was to restrict overall livestock numbers and output, and the arrangements will no doubt put at least a temporary halt to a further increase in enterprise size, even though transfer and leasing rules have been agreed.

Ewe premium (the annual headage payment from MAFF) is only paid subject to quota on up to 500 ewes on lowland farms and 1000 ewes in Less Favoured Areas (LFAs). The base year for calculating sheep quotas is 1991. Quota transfer cannot take place between lowland and upland farming areas. The special beef premium is only paid on the first 90 male cattle, provided stocking density rules are correctly adhered to.

The rules in respect of quota are fairly complex, and included in the calculation are all sheep and beef cattle numbers as well as any milk quota allocated to the holding.

HILL AND UPLAND AREAS

Although, as discussed above, beef cattle and sheep fulfil an important role in many farm situations, there are certain places where they play the major one. The best example is in the hill and upland regions of the UK, where the harsh climate, especially during the extended winter period, severely limits the production systems, livestock numbers and even the specific breed.

At the 'top of the hills', in the most exposed environment, where only the hardiest of plants such as heather and bent and fescue grasses can survive, equally hardy, specialised breeds of sheep such as the Scottish Blackface and Swaledale are to be found. Lambing takes place in late spring, ideally producing a single lamb, so that the ewe can provide an adequate milk supply, whilst at the same time regaining body weight lost during the previous winter. Hardiness and hefting are maintained by a policy of pure breeding using the same breed of ram as the ewes, and the female lambs or at least a

Upland sheep production

high proportion are retained in the flock. Older draft ewes are sold in the autumn to farms lower down the hill. Here cross-breeding can be undertaken to produce hybrid ewes for sale to lowland farms which are the main source of fat (meat) lambs. This progressive movement of suitable proven genetic material 'down the hill' in the sheep industry is known as stratification. It is one important justification for policy-makers supplementing the income of the hill farmer and so assisting to maintain this valuable source of breeding stock for the main lowland meat-producing flocks.

Although monetary support systems to beef and sheep enterprises will be discussed in more detail below, it is relevant at this point to draw attention to the part played by agricultural policy in retaining the farming activity of hill and upland holdings. Apart from the few farms with very large flocks, it is difficult for a hill sheep farmer to make a living selling only one lamb per year from each ewe. As already mentioned, the forage quality is inadequate for a ewe to produce twins, and higher stocking rates would produce over-grazing and lack of winter keep. Attempts were made with grant aid, especially in the 1950s and 60s, to improve sward quality and therefore stock-carrying capacity of the land by draining, liming, bracken control and even reseeding. These techniques, as well as being expensive, often proved to have a limited effective life and were criticised for destruction of the natural habitat, e.g. heather. In 1981, headage payments were introduced to assist in providing an adequate income for farmers. However, the Hill Livestock Compensatory Allowances (HLCAs) cause some concern, especially to environmentalists as payment is based on the number of stock carried on the farm, thus tending to encourage overstocking, which leads to overgrazing, damage to natural swards and even soil erosion.

Financial incentives in the form of contributions towards the cost of establishing diversified enterprises on such holdings were in place for several years but were withdrawn in 1993.

Although such things as pony trekking and bed and breakfast have been on offer to the public, the problems caused by the short summer season and the lack of essential resources, particularly capital and entrepreneurial skills, limit wider applicability of such ventures. Grouse shooting on many heather moors is now a major activity, with sheep grazing in these areas taking a less important, although necessary, part.

The current and likely future role of upland forestry in terms of employment opportunities for farmers and their families is of note, even if on a part-time basis. Suitably located woodland also provides shelter for stock and the shared use of forest roads by hill farmers leads to improved access for shepherds. Grant aid is available for the planting of shelter belts and small groups of trees with landscape value.

Beef cattle enterprises in the hills and uplands usually involve single sucklers, i.e. one cow rearing one calf per annum. Where outwintering is practised, hardiness in the cattle is essential, so requiring such breeds of cow as the Scottish Highland or Galloway. Spring calving in these herds is the norm. Unlike hill sheep, which can survive with minimal supplementary feed in winter, cattle depend upon the availability of silage, hay or other forages for survival. Capital grants in the 1950s–70s encouraged the provision of buildings for livestock and for feed storage in these less favoured areas. Such a facility not only allows feed wastage to be reduced but enables a change of cow type and calving date so that the output from the weaned calf can be considerably enhanced. Once winter housing is available, hardiness in the cow becomes far less important, so that milk production potential to feed the calf can be raised by using a beef cross dairy cow, one which is readily available as a by-product from the country's dairy herds. Summer or autumn calving also becomes feasible, as suckling continues during the housed period when there is a separate area for the calves to 'creep' into and obtain concentrate feed supplementation. Another potential benefit from investment in buildings for suckler beef, particularly when autumn calving is involved, is that breeding takes place in the winter, so that AI becomes practicable and use of semen from elite bulls is possible. With natural service, one bull is required for every 40 cows, and a less expensive sire of lower genetic potential is used. With AI, however, where a single bull sires thousands of calves, the cost of top-quality semen is not prohibitively high.

Overwintering of cattle in such environments frequently leads to considerable damage to the land, so that in some of the recently established ESAs (Environmentally Sensitive Areas), outwintering is not permitted, and the compensatory payments to producers take into consideration the extra costs involved in the provision of buildings.

LOWLAND SHEEP

A wide range of production systems exist for sheep enterprises on lowland farms. Some farmers do not breed but buy 'store' lambs from upland farms in the autumn and finish them for slaughter on specially grown forage crops throughout the winter. There is no quota restriction on such activity. A small number of farmers do not buy any animals but are paid on a headage basis to 'away winter' the ewe lambs of hill farmers on their beef or dairy holdings. Computerised data bases are in use to find the best match between providers and requirers of the service.

Those farmers with breeding flocks (which are the majority) plan for the most suitable breed of ewe and ram, together with date of lambing and feeding systems, to best meet the availability of farm resources as well as the needs of the market into which the output is to be sold. These flocks produce on average 160–190 lambs per 100 ewes mated, although a few may even rear more than 200%.

Specialist producers of breeding rams, for example, have pedigree flocks of meat-producing breeds such as Suffolks or Texels. These ewes lamb in early winter, usually indoors, so that by autumn the ram lambs are sufficiently well grown to be available to mate with the ewes in commercial flocks.

Early lambed flocks for meat production are carried predominantly on arable farms so using 'surplus' winter labour and buildings (following crop sales). Weaned lambs continue to be housed and are finished on a basically cereal diet for the early higher-priced market for spring lambs as at Easter. As the lambs are slaughtered at a young

Fat lambs

age (under four months) the male lambs do not need to be castrated (no behavioural or meat flavour problems). The dry ewes are then carried at high stocking rates on summer grassland, so minimising the competition with the arable enterprises on the farm. A small proportion of producers have a flock comprising a special type of sheep that is not dependent on photoperiodism to come into oestrus and breed. The Dorset Horn is such a breed and can produce a lamb crop every eight months. With such a system it is possible to divide the flock into two groups, each lambing frequently but staggered in time so that one group lambs every four months. In practice, however, the premium price received for 'out of season' lamb seldom covers the extra costs involved – a good example of where one can work with nature, but not against it!

The traditional ewe flock carried on an all-grass farm or even on an arable holding lambs in the spring (March/April) – ideally when the grass is beginning to grow. Housing is increasingly being used at lambing time as well as during late pregnancy to increase the efficiency of feeding, reduce labour and minimise lamb loss by being much more convenient for the shepherds. In order to provide the optimum welfare for the animals, the level of stockmanship with indoor lambing needs to be as high as, if not higher than, that of outdoor lambing. Competition for space when feeding, as well as during lambing, can cause stress on the ewes. Mismothering is much more likely to occur with tighter stocking density unless there is adequate supervision, coupled with the facility to separately pen each ewe and her lambs for one or two days until transfer to pasture.

GENERAL MANAGEMENT OF SHEEP

Codes of recommendations for the welfare of sheep made under the Agriculture (Miscellaneous Provision) Act 1968 are intended to encourage all those responsible for stock to adopt the highest standards of husbandry. As well as including general aspects of stockmanship, such as identifying and treating signs of ill-health, the recommendations cover aspects such as appropriate ventilation, floor surfaces, water provision and space allowances in buildings.

The main health problems of sheep are foot rot, parasitic worms of the gut and external parasites such as sheep scab and blowflies. Dipping with organophosphorus compound is effective against the external problems but some concern is being experienced in respect of the health of the people working with such chemicals. Sheep dipping to control scab is no longer compulsory, but MAFF is to introduce tighter controls at markets to prevent the movement of animals with the disease, which damages fleeces and hides. Farmers offering sheep infected with scab for sale may face fines up to £5000. An alternative to organophosphorus dips – ivermectin – has been licensed for use in the UK.

One recent technological development in the sheep industry which has positive animal welfare as well as financial implications is the electronic scanning of pregnant ewes in order to determine foetal numbers. Following a scan in mid-pregnancy, ewes can be penned and fed appropriately according to lamb numbers expected. This helps to minimise the lambing difficulty commonly associated with large single lambs and improves the survival rate of twins and multiples which with improved ewe nutrition have a higher birth weight.

Another interesting development which is increasingly applied to housed ewes is to shear the wool in the winter, soon after housing. This not only increases space availability but stimulates the ewe's appetite, so increasing average birth weight of lambs and therefore survivability.

Wool is normally removed from the sheep by shearing in early summer, when the weather is suitably mild and the new wool is

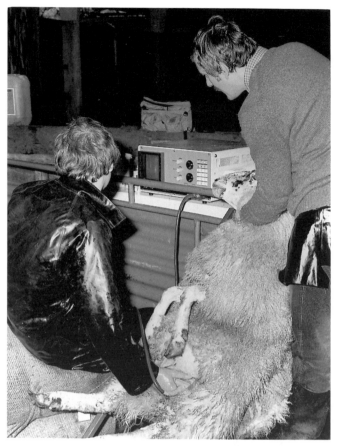

Pregnancy scanning of ewes (Courtesy of RASE)

starting to 'rise'. Over the centuries, wool was at times of major importance to the well-being of rural Britain. Today only some 7% of the income of a lowland flock comes from wool. Little can be done to improve quality other than by breeding and avoiding contamination of the fleece with organic matter such as hay and straw. The Wool Marketing Board is responsible for the collection, grading and marketing of all the product. Producers are paid from the 'pool' according to quantity and grade. The pool price is primarily determined by the world demand and supply, which is markedly influenced by the much larger producers from such countries as Australia and New Zealand. Much of the UK 'clip' is used for carpet manufacture.

LOWLAND BEEF PRODUCTION

In addition to the single suckler herds operated in the hills and uplands, there are a few herds on lowland grass and arable holdings. The ready availability of feed supplies on these farms has numerous advantages, although it may be necessary at times to limit the feed intake in order to avoid overfatness which leads to such problems as infertility and calving difficulties. The cost of feeding, especially in the arable situations, is often reduced by utilising by-products such as straw and 'waste' vegetables. Calving can be arranged to take place at any time (the cow not being subject to photoperiodism as with the ewe) but is usually determined by feed availability and the market requirement for the weaned calves.

Price support mechanisms have involved an annual headage payment for each suckler cow but since the 1992 CAP reforms, quotas have also been introduced (based on the numbers carried in 1992) and the scheme also takes into account stocking rates. Quotas, as with sheep, can be transferred along with land to a new owner without any reduction, but if there is a temporary transfer or leasing,

Multiple suckling (Courtesy of Dr P. J. Broadbent, Scottish Agricultural College)

15% is siphoned off into a national reserve for new entrants and special cases.

The importance of beef from the dairy herd was referred to in Chapter 3. Beef produced from suckled calves comprises 24% and together with the 7% from the culled beef cows represents one-third of the total output. The other two-thirds therefore originates from the dairy herd, 51% as beef reared calves (steers and heifers) and 13% from culled dairy cows. The final 5% is finished imported store cattle from Eire. The calves from the dairy herd comprise pure dairy bull calves (predominantly Holstein/Friesian), a few dairy heifers not required as replacements and particularly calves sired by a beef bull (heifers and bulls).

Until the Second World War, Ayrshires and Shorthorns were the predominant dairy breeds and did not produce particularly high-quality beef. Hereford and Aberdeen Angus were the most popular beef breeds, although not widely used in crossing with dairy cows. A marked turning point for UK beef production came in 1961 when MAFF agreed to the importation of Charolais cattle from Europe. Since then a range of other continental breeds have been introduced such as the Limousin, Simmental and Belgian Blue, which have been increasingly used both in suckler herds and in crossing programmes with dairy cows. The major advantages have been increased growth rates and yield of higher-quality meat from better conformation. Much more care is necessary when selecting appropriate sires for individual cows so as to avoid difficult calvings (dystocia) caused by big calves or those with wide shoulders or thighs.

The calves for beef production born in the dairy herd are reared on a wide range of systems. Some are sold in the first few weeks to specialised beef producers, whereas others stay on the dairy farm until after weaning and are reared along with the heifer replacement calves. All should receive colostrum – the first milk from the mother – for the first few days. The calves can then be transferred on to milk substitute fed from buckets or from teats connected to plastic bins or from automated dispensing machines. They are weaned at five to six weeks of age. A number of husbandry tasks need to be undertaken by skilled and trained stockpeople with particular attention to detail. Horn buds are removed (from horned breeds) involving the use of anaesthetic. Castration when required is normally undertaken in the early weeks of life following established codes of practice. Legislation (Veterinary Surgeon Act 1966) requires that animals over three months of age be castrated by a qualified veterinary surgeon. It will be explained below that entire (uncastrated) males can be satisfactorily reared in some systems of production, whereas steers

*Simmental cow and her nine calves—the result of embryo transfer (Courtesy of Dr
P. J. Broadbent, Scottish Agricultural College)*

(castrates) are needed for others.

A very small number of calves are reared in this country for veal, and some are exported for rearing in the veal industry of France, Italy, the Netherlands and Spain. Legislation is in place in respect of appropriate transportation for these animals, although implementation is left to the authority in the country involved. When calves are reared for veal, milk substitute is fed ad libitum for some 20 weeks to produce the light-coloured meat required by the trade. All such calves in the UK are now group housed in straw-bedded pens as the result of welfare legislation banning the use of veal crates. It is to be hoped that EU legislation will soon follow this British lead.

After weaning most beef calves are fed concentrates with hay or silage to appetite until three or even six months of age, depending upon the system of finishing to be used. There are three main rearing/finishing systems.

Cereal Beef

Known to most producers as barley beef, this is an intensive system which supplies an all-concentrate diet of 85% barley and 15% protein supplement provided on an ad lib basis from three months of age to slaughter at 11 to 13 months. The cattle are housed throughout their lives, so that year-round production and marketing are possible. This is appreciated by the meat trade which requires a constant supply of uniform-quality product, with a high lean meat content obtained by the early age of slaughter. Entire bulls can be used in this system as they are insufficiently mature to cause any of the taint problems in the meat which would be associated with older bulls. Safety is, of course, an important consideration when handling bulls of any age. Pens need to be constructed securely, fences to be at least 1.5 m high, warning signs erected and two stockmen present if and when it is necessary for one to enter the pen – for example, to supply straw bedding. Proprietary protein supplements usually contain an in-feed growth promoter, which modifies rumen fermentation, so increasing growth rate. In order to avoid bloat (excess gas production in the rumen), cattle should be provided with regular supplies of clean straw for bedding. They will eat some of this straw which, as well as helping rumen digestion, slightly reduces concentrate intake, thereby marginally lowering growth rate and so preventing excess stress on the animal's liver. A number of producers add a little chopped straw to the concentrate ration to prevent any liver damage and thus protect the valuable offal and also for welfare considerations.

Silage Beef

This is another intensive system of rearing which involves housing throughout, but using silage (grass or maize) as the major feed component. Growth rates are not as high as with cereal beef but if fast-growing continental-cross dairy bulls or steers are utilised, optimum carcase weights of 270 kg can be obtained before the animals reach 16 months of age. Welfare considerations, especially with bulls, require group size to be restricted to 20 animals. Regular weighing of the stock is necessary with this system so as to enable concentrate supplementation of the diet to be adjusted in order to maintain the required growth rate. Pen and handling area design is therefore critical if the stock are to be taken out, weighed and returned with minimal stress. These silage-based systems integrate well with a dairy farm where, for instance, stockmanship, silage and a good source of calves are available but perhaps milk quota or building suitability prevents economic expansion of the dairy herd. As with cereal beef, continuity of supply is possible, and due to newer techniques of butchery utilising heavier carcases used by the large multiples to provide ready-packed convenience products, this is a system of rearing encouraged by this sector of the trade.

Eighteen-Month Beef

As the name implies, the animals reared on this system average 18 months of age at slaughter. It is also known as the semi-intensive system of rearing as the animals spend a proportion of their rearing period at pasture. A typical system would be to use autumn-born beef cross dairy animals, either steers or heifers (not bulls). The cattle are reared indoors during the first winter from birth to 6 months, graze at pasture from 6 to 12 months and then are housed from 12 to 18 months for finishing on a range of diets. Such a system fits well with an arable farm as there are two groups of cattle in the winter and only one in the summer when the staff are more likely to be busy with the crop enterprises. A minimal area of grass is required for grazing of the young animals and a range of arable by-products including reject potatoes, misshaped carrots as well as silage will be available for finishing. Late-winter and spring-born calves fit better into an all-grass environment as two grazing seasons are commonly utilised with age at slaughter then increasing to 20 to 24 months. The main problem with grazing cattle tends to be parasitic worm infestation of the gut, which is controlled by administering anthelmintic medicines.

Following the 1992 CAP reforms of the beef sector, some producers have extended the rearing period beyond 18 months in order to be eligible for the second beef premium after 22 months of age (detailed below). This involves either extending a winter finishing period with some grazing or bringing cattle indoors at the end of a normal grass finishing period.

HANDLING

With all cattle and sheep, it is important to ensure minimal stress on the stock when drawing out (selecting) for slaughter, loading and transporting to the abattoir. Again, legislation (1975 Special Order) covers cleanliness of transport vehicles and appropriate restraining during transport. Good management and stockmanship with handling can, however, improve the conditions for the stock over and above those specified by the law. Effective communication with the abattoir in respect of ideal time of arrival will, for instance, minimise the time spent by the animals in the holding pens before slaughter.

This is particularly important with the bull beef, as any stress or excitement (such as penning next to heifers or cows in the lairage) will cause the meat to have a higher pH (be less acidic) and to be dark in colour, dry and too firm in texture, so reducing value.

PRICE SUPPORT

The major source of income for the beef producers is, of course, the value of the carcase – which is affected by weight, conformation, breed, sex and season (variable supply/demand).

From the 1950s additional make-up payments were received from the government, and since the UK joined the EC in 1974 these have been part of a wider European system. Intervention buying has been the main aspect of EC policy, involving purchasing and cold storage of specified quantities and categories of beef and then returning this to the market when prices are high. In practice, the system has been an expensive failure, with stocks being sold into the world market aided by costly export subsidies after long periods of storage. The special beef premium was introduced in 1989 and producers receive

Sale by auction

a single headage payment on a maximum of 90 male cattle (bulls or steers) each year. Since the CAP reforms of 1992 the special premium is paid at 10 months of age and again at 22 months (if not slaughtered by that age). In order to reduce fraudulent claims, each animal must have an Individual Document – commonly known as a 'passport'.

The price support policy for sheep farmers is similar, with earlier compensatory payments now replaced by a ewe premium which is paid annually on each ewe quota with maximum limits of 500 (1000 in LFAs).

THE FUTURE

Producers of beef and sheepmeat will obtain an increasing proportion of their income directly from the market place so there will be a need to modify the genetic potential of the animals, along with feeding and management practices to meet the specific needs of the buyers. Research and development will continue to guide producers towards optimum methods of breeding, rearing, meat handling post-slaughter and butchering to improve eating quality, especially flavour. Although a small proportion of the population, mainly young people, are non-meat-eaters, future consumption levels will be influenced not just by value for money and eating quality of the meat but by the impression consumers have as to how farmers and slaughterers care for their animals. Improved training of stock-people, together with good physical facilities, will enable animals to be reared and handled in a less stressful environment. EU policy – using subsidies and stocking rate limits to reverse the recent trends to intensive beef and sheep systems – will encourage more extensive systems.

CHAPTER FIVE

Pigs and Poultry

INTRODUCTION

The production of pig and poultry meat, together with eggs, is another important aspect of the UK agricultural industry. Together in 1991 they represented some 16% of the total output of UK agriculture. Finished pigs currently generate £950m per annum, eggs £440m, broiler meat £600m and turkey £300m.

Although a wide range of production systems are in use – from intensive, fully housed and environmentally controlled enterprises to extensive systems such as outdoor pig production, all tend to use less land than cattle and sheep enterprises. Pigs and poultry, being non-ruminants, cannot efficiently digest grass and forages and so require diets based predominantly on cereals and protein feeds. As pig and poultry enterprises can produce high outputs from a small area of land they have, over the years, been ideally suited to the small family farm. However, the trend, especially with poultry but also with pig finishing, has in recent years been towards larger-scale units (more like an industrial process) controlled by a smaller number of producers. One important reason for the development of such large units has been the absence of any production quotas or government price-support systems. As the total supply of product so often matches or is in excess of the requirements of the market, prices and therefore profit levels are kept low so that only the larger efficient producers are better placed to survive. This type of situation stimulates closer integration between different sectors of the food chain, for example in egg production between the hatchery, feed supplier, egg packer and wholesaler.

The future profitability of production for many pig and poultry farmers will be adversely affected as capital investment is required for the modification or replacement of facilities to meet the increasingly rigorous welfare regulations. Additional financial pressure will exist if food products are imported into the UK from countries where the cost of production is lower because the same EU regulations are not enforced effectively.

Although some breeds of both pigs and poultry still exist in the wild, the modern types have been domesticated over many years and developed to be much more efficient converters of food into a saleable product. Pigs in particular, but also young chicks, need to be protected from extremes of temperature, which is done by housing systems. Housing also protects the animals from predators, e.g. the fox and even from wild birds which can carry and spread disease.

LOCATION

Pig and poultry enterprises have traditionally been established in areas within easy access to the ports because of their earlier dependence for feeding stuffs from imported cereals and proteins. Such examples are poultry in Lancashire (Liverpool docks and the Manchester Ship Canal) and pigs in North Humberside (Hull) or Essex (Tilbury). In more recent years, aided by EC support, more home-grown cereals (wheat and barley) have been produced, a proportion being available to replace the imported commodities, especially maize. Some 55% of the wheat grown in the UK for livestock feeding is consumed by pigs and poultry. Many of the older feed mills established earlier in the century at the dockside have now been replaced by modern, much more automated mills located in arable areas and often near motorway junctions. Town and Country Planners as well as rural residents have become increasingly concerned about the location of intensive units in terms of smell, noise from fans and from animals when feeding, as well as dust from feathers and bedding materials. It is therefore in the interest of producers to locate new units well away from homes (apart from those occupied by stock supervisors) to avoid these problems. Operating a livestock unit which is located in the centre of an arable farm eases the logistics of manure handling and spreading on the land.

The location of production units in an isolated site also helps to minimise the incidence of disease spread from other animals or from casual visitors such as sales representatives. Modern units commonly have a vermin-proof fence and facilities for lorries to blow feed into holding bins and for animals to be loaded via a ramp on the perimeter of the unit to avoid lorries entering and possibly bringing in disease.

TRANSPORTATION

Optimum location of abattoirs, processing plants and packing stations is also an important consideration within the industry. Minimising the time animals spend in transit has obvious welfare implications. It is also critical to efficient transportation of the processed products to the market – increasingly to the regional distribution centres of the multiple retailers.

The regulations in respect of transporting pigs (as well as other livestock) from farm to abattoir have increased in complexity in recent years. The Welfare of Animals during Transit Order 1992 is enforced by the County Trading Standards Officers. Hauliers find to their dismay a wide variation in the interpretation of the order from one county to another. Space requirement within the lorry is a key factor, as are cleanliness before loading and the maximum travelling time allowed. Particular problems arise in this latter area as the Ministry of Transport has regulations in respect of drivers' hours. A lorry driver may spend considerable time travelling between farms and in loading the animals; then before arriving at the abattoir he finds that his hours are used so has to stop for a rest period. This may be advantageous for the driver but not for the animals – particularly on hot days. Some hauliers therefore use a pair of drivers – one who collects and loads an articulated trailer and the other who then delivers the load to the slaughter plant.

All animals are now checked on arrival at the abattoir by a veterinary surgeon, who therefore has considerable influence on the conditions operated by the haulier. Loading and unloading pigs can be a frustrating task requiring patience and understanding of animal behaviour. Electric prods are sometimes necessary but their use should be minimised to avoid stressing the animals.

PIG PRODUCTION SYSTEMS

The primary role of UK pig enterprises is to supply the market requirement for pig meat every week of the year. Before household refrigerators became commonplace, pig meat sales were regularly depressed in the warmer summer months and only picked up when there was an R in the month! The current market requires a range of weights of finished pigs according to the specific needs of the fresh pork, bacon or processed product sectors.

Many pig farmers operate both breeding and finishing enterprises, whereas others specialise in breeding and sell weaners or store pigs to other farmers who have more appropriate resources for finishing. Breeding is a suitable enterprise for a small farm whereas much more land is required to take the considerable quantities of manure produced from a finishing unit.

Pigs tend to be more susceptible to disease than ruminants, especially to viral and bacterial infections of the lungs, intestines and female breeding tracts. Farmers who regularly buy pigs for finishing prefer to obtain their supplies from one breeder in order to prevent cross-infections by mixing stock from several farms. The movement of pigs from farm to farm is a cause for concern when there is an outbreak of virulent disease such as swine fever, so the local authority has to be notified of all movements and permits issued. No pigs – not even those kept as rare breeds or pets – may be moved without a permit.

Breeding Stock

Up to the 1960s a high proportion of the breeding sows were pure breds of such breeds as the Large White and Landrace. It was common practice to mate the sows with a boar of another breed, so producing cross-bred meat animals which grew well. Replacement gilts were normally home-bred, being obtained by using a boar of the same breed to serve the better sows in the herd.

In the early 1960s a group of pig farmers in and around Oxfordshire and Berkshire agreed to cooperate in measuring and recording the performance of their animals so as to identify the sows that not only produced the most piglets but also the litters with the highest growth rate and feed conversion efficiency. Having been identified, these elite sows were served by the most outstanding boars available to produce offspring with the highest genetic potential. In order to break the cycle of disease which normally spreads from the sows to the piglets, hysterectomy of the sows was undertaken and the piglets were removed surgically from the uterus. The baby pigs were placed in an incubator, fed artificially and then reared in new (disease-free) buildings. This technique produced minimal disease (MD) pigs, which were then multiplied up to produce large numbers of healthy pigs, which eventually allowed re-stocking of all the farms of the cooperative members. This was the first pig breeding company – setting the trend followed today by most commercial pig breeders, who buy their stock from such organisations. The particular 'types' vary somewhat from one company to another but for normal indoor systems they are predominantly hybrids of the Landrace and Large

White breeds incorporating, for example, a small proportion of Duroc or Hampshire blood. The special hardy stock required for outdoor systems may include a proportion of genetics from the Wessex breed, which produces offspring which provide quality meat.

Boars are also supplied from the companies according to a points scheme which evaluates their growth rate and feed efficiency, together with the lean meat content, which is measured electronically using a scanning device over the muscles of the shoulder and loin. Artificial insemination has been available for many years but has been much slower in receiving acceptability with pig farmers than dairy farmers.

It is more difficult to maintain excellent health in outdoor systems as the pigs can pick up infection from birds and other wild animals. As mentioned above, it is very worthwhile for pigs kept indoors to be protected as much as possible from such sources of infection. Some very high health status herds require all members of staff as well as the veterinary surgeon to shower when coming in and going out of the unit and have special working clothing. No visitors are allowed into these units.

Production Cycle

Replacement gilts, which are normally purchased at 5 to 6 months of age, join the breeding herd when 8 to 9 months old and weighing 90–100 kg, so replacing the sows which need to be culled (on average after some 6 to 8 litters). Sows to be retained are served after 7 to 10 days following the weaning of their last litter and are in 'in-pig' for approximately 114 days (3 months, 3 weeks and 3 days). Feeding levels during pregnancy are critical, as litter size and weight are related to the sow's body condition. When housed in groups, sows tend to fight and bully each other especially at feeding time, so it is preferable to have individual feeding stalls or adequate space so that appropriate feed levels can be given. As herds have increased in size over the last 20 years, special 'dry' sow housing facilities have been developed to minimise the chores of feeding and manure handling. Such an example is stall housing in which each sow has an individual narrow pen or stall in which she is not only fed but spends all her time during the pregnancy period. Temperature and ventilation can be readily controlled and good observation by stock people is possible, in addition to accurate, individual feeding. From a welfare point of view, however, the system is far from ideal, as the animals have minimal room to move and exercise. EU legislation (Welfare of Pigs 1991) prohibits the installation of any new stall or tethering systems and will ban the use of existing systems from the end of 1998. Group housing of pregnant sows in straw-bedded pens will therefore become more popular again, and possibly with the feeding taking place in special walk-through stalls where rationing is electronically controlled by individual transponders fitted into tags in the sows' ears.

As the sow approaches farrowing (giving birth), she is usually moved to another specialised house which is fitted with farrowing crates, which are designed to restrain her from overlaying and crushing the piglets. Although she is somewhat restricted in movement, the crate is sufficiently wide to allow her to recline in such a way that all the teats are exposed for suckling. At each side of the

Modern electronically controlled sow feeding (RASE)

crate there is usually an area especially for use by the piglets, known as the 'creep', which is kept at a higher temperature in order to attract the pigs, when not suckling, away from the mother. A number of larger breeding units arrange for their veterinarian to inject a batch of sows with a hormone and so induce the births to take place at specific times – a technique also widely used in hospital maternity units. This justifies the provision of additional help to be on duty during reasonable hours to supervise farrowing. It involves removing the piglets at birth into a special warm box and returning an appropriate number to each sow when she has completed farrowing. In this way welfare is enhanced as post-natal deaths are reduced and sows suckle the number of piglets best matched to their milk production potential – so reducing variability in size at weaning.

Although many years ago weaning took place at 8 weeks after birth, in the 1970s it was reduced to 5 weeks, and in most herds is now down to 21–25 days. This enables a sow to have 2.4 litters each year, and so if 10 piglets are reared in the average litter, she produces 24 piglets per year. Even earlier weaning has been tried by some producers, but the baby piglets are particularly vulnerable to temperature change and require a very sophisticated and expensive diet.

Specialised housing for weaned pigs even at 3 weeks of age is required incorporating temperature control and well-designed feeding troughs and water drinkers. The diet for such animals needs to be particularly palatable as well as high in energy and in protein. As the pig grows, the ration can be progressively reduced in protein level, so lowering the cost of liveweight gain.

Numerous housing systems are in use for subsequent rearing and finishing. Some designs include insulated floors which require no bedding materials and many have a part or all of the pen incorporating slatted floors for efficient removal of dung and urine to an underground store. Straw-based systems which were popular some 20 to 30 years ago when labour costs were lower are once again increasing in popularity. It is now possible to use mini-tractors and swivel loaders to quickly and effectively clean out the manure and straw between each batch of animals. The general perception is that pigs housed on straw are less stressed, so the pig meat is of higher quality and thus may in the future earn a premium price from the customer.

Pigs being finished for the pork market are usually fed ad lib but to obtain premium grades, most bacon pigs need to have their feeds restricted. Mechanisation and automation of feeding are increasing, not only to reduce the chore of the task but to enable more frequent feeding, which is coupled with improved digestion and growth. Liquid feeding is often involved so allowing numerous by-products from the food industry such as whey and skimmed milk to be included in diets. The feeding of swill (waste feed from catering establishments), once very widely undertaken, is now strictly controlled, having to be steam-sterilised before use. The feeding of food products such as bread and cakes which have passed their 'sell by' date is widely practised.

A weaner 'pool' with straw bedding and ad-lib feeding

Weighing of pigs as they approach finishing weight is a necessity especially for those on contract for a bacon factory as uniformity of pig is essential for uniformity of the finished product. Careful handling to avoid stress is yet another aspect of good stockmanship.

Outdoor Weaner Production

Although the extensive system of keeping sows is currently very topical and is certainly increasing in popularity, it is not new. In the 1950s when pig production began to increase following contraction during wartime due to shortage of cereals for livestock feeding, outdoor rearing systems were widely used. Wooden arks, fitted with an outside 'run', were located on pasture and moved forward by towing with a tractor several times each week, in this way adding fertility to the land.

The development towards managing larger batches of sows together, controlled by electrified fencing, and sheltering as well as farrowing in simple, semi-circular shaped huts, also took place in the 1950s and 1960s. Richard Roadnight who farmed on the light chalkland soils of the Oxfordshire downs was such a pioneer. He crossed Wessex Saddleback sows with a Large White boar to produce a hybrid sow known as a 'Britwell Blue', which formed the basis of his outdoor breeding herd. These were crossed with another white boar to produce the slaughter generation. The whole group of sows was arranged to farrow twice a year (weaning at 8 weeks of

Outdoor sows under ideal conditions (Courtesy of RASE)

age) in the spring and autumn – so avoiding young pigs on hand during the worst of the winter weather.

The 1980s and 1990s version of the outdoor system involves using the latest hybrid females specially bred for the conditions by the breeding companies. The offspring from this stock matches the needs of the pig meat market but the sows are still hardy and productive. The current trend is to subdivide the herd into several groups with one batch farrowing each week, followed by weaning at 3 to 4 weeks. On the surface, the system would appear to be more welfare-friendly than the intensive, fully housed system but that is not really the situation. The extremes of weather experienced in the field can be quite stressful to the stock as well as to the pig staff! It is very depressing to find one or more piglets from a litter frozen to the ground. Very wet or frosty, cold weather understandably causes considerable problems; both can be minimised by liberal use of straw bedding within the huts. High summer temperatures are often as stressful to the sows, affecting appetite, milk supply and therefore piglet performance. Attempts to build temporary shades are seldom successful; the preferable solution is to dig a hole, fill it with water and allow the sows to wallow.

A man-made wallow

Some developments in the design of portable buildings better suited to the rearing of young pigs at pasture have also been undertaken. Ad lib feeding is incorporated and for the majority of the year reasonable animal performance is obtained. Growth rate and feed conversion efficiency can, however, be affected by extremes of weather. Nevertheless, some farmers are keen to develop such 'green' systems and hope to receive a supplement on the price when the animals are sold. The meat from such systems is currently supplying a niche in the market which would soon become over-supplied if too many producers changed to this system.

POULTRY PRODUCTION SYSTEMS

The sight of a few hens scratching around in the farmyard, although commonplace up to the 1950s, is now somewhat rare. The poultry industry has developed rapidly since that time, leading the way for other sectors of agriculture in terms of improved genetics, nutrition and management systems.

Although a few farms still retain a small flock of laying birds – perhaps to supply a retail outlet or farm shop, the poultry industry is increasingly moving into the hands of a few large companies. Eggs for hatching are produced on contract, large-scale automated hatcheries operate continuously and chicks for both egg production and poultry meat are reared in large-scale enterprises often linked (in business terms) to a feed manufacturer. The two main sectors of poultry meat and eggs are quite distinct and usually operate on separate sites with different breeds and strains of bird, feeding and housing systems.

Egg Production

There are some 33 million laying hens in the UK producing an annual sum of £440 million. The predominant market is for eggs with a brown shell, as these are considered more robust and of a higher quality than white eggs. Surprisingly, the opposite situation applies in many other countries such as the USA, where almost all the eggs sold have white shells. Special hybrid birds have been developed by international breeding companies which can produce up to 300 eggs in a 12-month laying period. Following hatching, chicks are sexed and the day-old pullets (female chicks) are boxed and transported to rearing farms. Here they are usually reared 'on the floor' with wood shavings as litter in a house with controlled temperature, ventilation and lighting. The modern hybrid pullet matures more rapidly than its predecessor, starting to lay at 9 months of age. Some pullets are reared in special cages, in which it is rather more difficult for stock people to observe them. However, there is less competition for feed

Outdoor pullet rearing in the 1930s

space, and if they are to be housed in cages for laying, they will already be accustomed to the system. During the rearing period, the birds are vaccinated against the diseases they are most likely to be affected by, such as Newcastle disease.

Numerous designs of housing and management systems for laying birds have been developed, each with its pros and cons. The most common are tiered cages three levels high. The floors of the cages are constructed of wire mesh through which the droppings fall. The floor slopes slightly towards the front of the cage so that the eggs roll into a trough at the front. Food is offered on an ad lib basis in well-designed, automatically topped-up feeding troughs, and water comes from automatic drinkers – at least two in each cage, in case of a failure or blockage. In larger units, the water supply is metered to each block of cages, monitored and recorded daily, as a fall-off in consumption is the first sign to the stockpeople of any ill health in the flock. Most units also have automatic egg conveyors on the front of the cages which not only transfer the eggs carefully

Intensive egg production

along for grading but also have a trip mechanism to count the production from each tier.

There is little doubt that such a system produces clean, specifically known date-of-lay eggs from healthy birds receiving an optimum nutritional input. The major problem is that of welfare, as birds in multi-occupation of 4 or 5 per cage have minimal space to exercise and exhibit natural behaviour. Considerable research and development is under way to provide improved cages but it is interesting to observe, for example, that when given the choice, birds prefer to stand on a wire mesh (as on a branch in the wild) rather than on a mat or rubber cushion. The Welfare of Battery Hens Regulations 1987 laid down minimum standards for stocking densities and cage design. This legislation applied to any new cages installed after

1 January 1988 and will affect all installations after 1 January 1995.

An alternative housing system which has some welfare advantages is the deep litter system. As the name implies, the floor of the house is covered with litter in which the birds can scratch. Food and water are available, and nest boxes are provided for egg laying. Not all the birds use the boxes, so stockpeople have to look out for and collect eggs laid in the (dirty?) litter. Some fighting and tail-feather-pulling often take place, so not all the birds can be described as stress-free.

In order to reduce the capital cost per bird by increasing the stocking density of the building above that of the deep litter system, banks of perches can be installed – a system known as a barn house. Some of the same vices exist as in deep litter and it is more difficult for stockpeople to move around in the house to check the birds.

As with weaner pig production, extensive free-range systems have been developed, primarily to meet the demands of customers who are prepared to pay a premium for eggs produced in this way. Houses with nesting boxes, feed hoppers and water are commonly located within a fenced area of grassland. This area can be divided, into two or more pens for use in rotation as and when one becomes damaged and dirty because of wet conditions. Predator control is a major task, as the fox considers such a system to be a challenge and

Modern free-range egg production (Courtesy of RASE)

usually wins! Numerous types of protective devices are used, including electrified fences, but most producers go to the trouble of locking in the birds from dusk to dawn. The average mortality of free-range hens from all causes is about 10% per annum.

Poultry Meat Production

In terms of consumption, poultry meat is one of the major success stories in UK agriculture. The average person now eats some 8 oz per week in comparison with 5 oz beef and 3 oz lamb. Not only do consumers consider poultry meat to be good value for money but it meets the increasing requirement for diets with low levels of cholesterol. As with egg production, the widespread uptake of improved genetics, optimum diets and efficient housing systems has enabled the cost of producing poultry meat to be kept competitive. Ducks, geese and turkeys are also an important sector of the industry, although they tend to be much more influenced by seasonality and by the Christmas trade in particular.

As with egg production, a few international companies also dominate the supply of chicks for this sector of the industry.

On-floor rearing of turkeys

Breeding stock are contracted to supply hatching eggs to produce broiler chicks (the name given to chickens reared for meat). Both male and female chicks are reared, often together when a range of carcase weights are required or in separate groups if the market needs uniform weights.

All are reared 'on the floor' and stay together as a group during the rearing period, receiving ad lib feed and water. One of the main reasons contributing to the low cost of poultry meat is the fact that the birds grow so quickly and convert the feed so efficiently, being ready for the market by 8 weeks of age. After the 'harvest' of the crop, the house is cleaned out, washed, disinfected and rested for a week before the next batch of day-old chicks arrive. In this way each house can be used for over 5 batches of birds per year – so reducing the cost of capital per bird produced.

The need for well-trained experienced staff is again vital, as with good stockmanship few problems occur. Optimum lighting is an example of the need for production control, as if too bright, the birds tend to fight and if too dim, observation is more difficult.

Environmentally controlled housing systems for both pigs and poultry, but particularly for broilers, are very dependent upon the power supply to maintain air flow by ventilation. In all units, but especially where power cuts are common, some back-up system is essential, as birds can quickly smother in hot weather. A stand-by generator is the ideal solution. Less costly is the installation of magnetically attached panels which fall off when the power is lost, so that natural ventilation takes over until the power is restored. These are further examples of the concern that farmers have for their stock – not just for economic reasons but because they have a real concern for their welfare.

CONCLUSION

There is little doubt that continued technical developments in the breeding, feeding, housing, processing and marketing aspects of production will stimulate further improvements in efficiency. Pig and poultry products are relatively easy to transport, so that one can envisage increased world trade – especially from those countries with a lower cost of production. Following the GATT agreements in 1994, the USA, for example, will be looking towards the EU market to supply frozen chicken. As the financial pressure increases on UK pig and poultry farmers, this will have a roll-on effect on cereal producers, who are increasingly dependent upon the consumption of their output by intensive livestock enterprises.

It is to be hoped that UK customers will in the future be prepared to pay a marginally higher price for eggs, pig and poultry meat that has been home produced on well-managed farms of high welfare status.

CHAPTER SIX

Other Influences

We have seen that the agricultural and food industry in the UK, whilst being driven more and more by market forces, is also under the major influences of economic, social and regulatory pressures. The industry has operated under a controlled regime for many years; indeed, few people farming today will have had direct experience of the depression and free market between the two world wars. Milk producers, having sold all their milk to the Milk Marketing Board for 60 years, are now faced with making new arrangements, as are potato producers with the Potato Marketing Board due to be abolished in three years' time. Farmers are now facing a move towards a free market economy, closer to world prices for many commodities, and any support is linked to crop area rather than to volume of production.

COUNTRYSIDE CONSERVATION

Concern about the environment and a desire to conserve 'traditional' countryside features has led to a plethora of schemes designed to encourage farmers to take more interest in conservation. These schemes are voluntary, sometimes complementary to one another, sometimes overlapping, some available to all, others confined to specified areas. They are often administered by different bodies, and grants may be discretionary or as of right. It has been suggested that there should be some rationalisation between the schemes and their administration, but the government attitude is that a 'menu' of schemes widens the choice of individual farmers and enables them to choose what is best for their personal circumstances.

An example of a scheme tied to specified locations is that of the Environmentally Sensitive Areas (ESAs). These are designed to specifically encourage farming practices which will help to maintain and enhance the environment. ESAs seek to ensure that in some of the most valued countryside economic pressures will not damage landscapes or historic features. In these areas farmers who are willing to carry out environmentally beneficial practices are offered payments to help offset pressures to use intensive production methods and to carry out positive management of environmental features.

The Farm Woodland Scheme, on the other hand, is an example available to all farmers, but with payments varying as to location and types of woodland planted. This scheme is designed to encourage farmers throughout the country to plant new woodland on land currently in agriculture. Such tree planting will divert land from agricultural production, enhance the landscape and create wildlife habitats. It will, in the long run, contribute homegrown timber for use on the farm or as a source of fuel and it will improve sporting interests. Native trees are encouraged, although some species of conifers are allowed as a 'nurse' crop.

There has been much concern over the loss of hedgerows. Not all losses can be attributed to farmers, as hedges are often removed because of building work and road widening. Hedges and field boundaries are an important feature of the British landscape, and their total length was estimated at 1.5 million km in 1990. To the farmer a hedge provides shelter for livestock and acts as a barrier. But hedges are expensive to maintain. In the past when farms carried a large work force, labour was available to trim hedges and to maintain them by laying or coppicing. Such labour is not available today, and hedges are trimmed mechanically. Some hedges have become relic hedges, rows of trees or shrubs and no longer stock-proof. The 1990 Countryside Survey estimated that about 6% of hedges were of this type and that the length of such relic hedges had increased by 55% since 1984. During the same period 23% fewer hedges were recorded but not all these had been removed, as relic hedges were counted as lost. There has been some new planting, often associated with management for game shooting, and grants are available to help with the costs of planting new hedges.

Changes in hedges and field boundaries are largely due to economic pressures on farmers, which leave them with little choice but to reduce the length of hedgerows where possible and to use machines for trimming.

Grant schemes linked to environmental objectives certainly help to encourage farmers, the people who actually manage the land, to take an interest in their farms which is wider than just the production of crops and stock. The schemes are aimed at enhancing the appearance of the countryside and helping wildlife. In some cases grants are available only if the results of the improvement can be seen and enjoyed by the public – perhaps from a road or a viewpoint.

ACCESS

One aspect which creates problems which are difficult to resolve is that of access to the countryside. Walking, whether long or short distances, is a very popular activity, and footpath access is a right and privilege which is zealously guarded. Footpaths which cross fields were originally established to allow local people to get to work, to church or to the village. Today they are used by visitors who may not always understand country ways and farming needs. Some farms have fields with several footpaths across them, and this creates problems when grazing certain classes of stock. For instance, if a footpath runs through a field, only bulls of beef breeds are allowed to graze, and they must be accompanied by cows or heifers. A cow with a calf at foot, or even a ewe with lambs, can also be aggressive when faced with strangers, especially if they are accompanied by a dog. Footpaths are a statutory right of way and must be maintained and kept open. There are strict rules and regulations covering this, and they are usually observed, although a few farmers neglect their obligations and cause problems.

There is a demand for open access to all countryside, except where crops are growing. This would mainly affect open moorland and is resisted by moor owners in the interests of sheep farming and grouse shooting and by some conservation bodies concerned about possible disturbance to wildlife.

Farmers who have planted woodland and those who have long-term set-aside are encouraged to allow public access for recreation, perhaps for payment. Some farms and estates provide access for horse riding on a fee-paying basis, welcomed by riders as offering safe, pleasant riding away from busy roads.

This is a new form of land use, a development watched with interest. The Country Landowners Association (CLA), recognising the changing nature of demand for access to the countryside, has proposed the formation of Countryside Recreation and Access Groups. These groups would ensure better communications by bringing together landowners, occupiers, user groups, local authorities and statutory agencies. Such groups would define the needs of those seeking access for recreation or sporting activities and seek to ensure that positive efforts are made to develop opportunities whilst taking into account the needs of primary land users and local communities.

Headlands of set-aside fields can supplement farm tracks as areas for horse riding (Courtesy of RASE)

In some parts of the country farm accommodation has been offered for many years, and this practice is spreading and growing rapidly. It is a way of maintaining or raising farm incomes and an example of farm diversification. MAFF introduced the Farm Diversification Scheme in 1988 to provide financial assistance for farmers intending to diversify their farm businesses. Not surprisingly, farm-based bed and breakfast and self-catering enterprises are concentrated in the west of England and Wales. Fewer farms offer accommodation and recreation in eastern counties such as Lincolnshire, where the farms are larger and predominantly arable and there is less demand.

ALTERNATIVE ENTERPRISES

Conventional farming is concerned with the production of food and fibre which will not be processed on the farm but will be sold as raw materials to the food and manufacturing industries. In seeking to obtain a greater share of the market, some farmers will look for alternatives to basic farming. It is not always easy to develop these alternatives, as extra skills are required which may not already be available; establishing new market outlets and planning controls may also present problems. A small alternative enterprise may be acceptable, but if it is successful and wishes to expand, then it may face objections from local residents and planners, who will argue that it does not fit into their conception of the countryside.

The main groups of alternative enterprises are:

1. *Tourism and recreation*, providing accommodation, camping and activity holidays, to which may be added visitor centres, riding, farm museums and field sports, such as shooting and fishing.

   This might, perhaps, be the place to consider the influence which field sports have on the countryside and its wildlife and on rural employment. Direct expenditure on countryside sports by organisers and those taking part is £1.4 billion per annum, and 65,000 full-time job equivalents are directly associated with these activities. Countryside sports produce fish, game meat, venison and horn, and about 50% is sold, the rest being consumed by those taking part or their friends. The total value of produce sold is worth about £17.5 million. Country sports contribute an element of stability to the structure of rural communities. They attract broad support from the main social groups and from all ages; the rural employment which they generate impacts upon hotels and other centres, and this is especially important in remoter areas.

   Countryside sports provide some of the management tools responsible for maintaining the beauty of the landscape. The providers and participants contribute to the upkeep of large parts of the countryside which is enjoyed by urban and country people and overseas visitors. Much of this activity is voluntary and at no public cost.

   Heather moorland and the wildlife it supports depend on successfully balancing multiple land uses by healthy sheep and grouse populations and heather, maintained as a crop through cyclical burning.

   In arable areas, conservation headlands, which involve the selection and restrictive use of herbicides and fungicides on the margins of cereal fields, greatly improve the numbers of game birds reared. They also benefit butterflies, songbirds and wild flowers. The average grey partridge covey size has been increased from two to six chicks per brood and pheasant brood size more than doubled. There are either very small reductions in cereal yields or none at all. Conservation headlands are widely established and are making an important contribution to wildlife and landscape, especially in the areas where intensive cereal farming became popular during the 1960s.

Research has shown that farmers with an interest in game shooting spend 25% more on landscape improvement than those without interest. Shooting interests also exerted a strong influence on the reasons given by occupiers of small woods as a reason for retaining and planting them.

Farmers and landowners provide access to game and coarse fishing, either directly or through letting to fishing clubs. Large ponds and lakes, rivers and canals can be managed for good fishing and make a useful addition to farm income.

Those providing and taking part in countryside sports devote special attention to maintaining and creating healthy habitats, including clean waters and streams, rivers and lakes. The attractiveness of the British landscape owes much to their commitments and many more benefit than those who participate in the sports.

2. *Adding value to products.* This may involve direct selling to the public of meat and meat products, dairy products and milled cereals. Pick-your-own fruit and vegetables is popular where the holding is close to centres of population and has good road access. Such enterprises can be successful even on a small scale but must comply with all relevant regulations. Expansion of a successful business may run into difficulties if located in or near a village.

   Adding value can be big business and there are a number of dairy enterprises which provide milk and dairy products on a large scale, either home brand or under the name of a retailer. One unusual, and successful, example from the arable sector is a farm which processes all its wheat for sale as dog biscuits. Adding value is not a universal panacea, as much depends on the enterprise, enthusiasm and skills of the owner, but it can bring more of the market return to the producers.

3. *Unusual enterprises.* These will depend on the interests and skills of the individual, locating the market outlet and, in many cases, the location of the farm. Some produce sheep milk for what is a limited market, as is keeping deer or goats to produce venison and goat meat. Rare breeds may provide an interest for visitors

while also helping to maintain certain breeds of livestock for future generations.

The market for organic produce is limited but can be supplied by specialist producers prepared to devote the necessary care and attention to the system.

Non-food crops, some of which can be grown on set-aside land, are of limited interest but can be grown successfully with the right soil and climate. Linseed is the most widely seen but can be difficult to harvest in a wet autumn. Evening primrose (*Oenothera biennis*), grown for its oil, has been introduced on some farms and, under licence, 600 ha of hemp were grown for fibre in 1993. These crops and others often make the headlines in the popular press but are of no real significance to the economics of the industry, although they may be important to individual farmers.

An enterprise which has developed successfully is growing Christmas trees, usually as a sideline, although for some it is a major occupation. Lawn turf too is produced on a few farms.

There is a considerable interest in alternative crops for non-food use. Potentially there are market opportunities for crops for fuel, fibre and paper-making and for building materials. However, there are problems in developing these markets, as the capital costs of processing plants are high, and while other EU governments have provided assistance, the UK government has not done so. North

Growing lawn turf

An alternative enterprise—producing wildflower seed

Sea oil makes this country less concerned about fuel supplies than those with little or no indigenous sources of fossil fuel.

Bio fuels such as bio-diesel and ethanol might replace 2 or 3% of the fuel oil market but this would represent a significant area of land. Some European countries are using bio-diesel, and one hectare of oilseed rape yielding 3 tonnes of seed would produce 1 tonne of oil, enough to power a diesel car for a year. The energy balance is, perhaps, not quite so attractive, as growing the oilseed rape would use energy for cultivations and harvesting together with fertilisers and chemical sprays to control pests. Carbon dioxide produced from burning the oil would be recycled from that 'fixed' by the growing crop and would not involve the release of fossil carbon dioxide.

Short rotation coppice could also make a contribution to energy supplies. Poplar or willow should, after five years, produce 12 tonnes of dry matter per hectare. A small 8 megawatt power station would require 40,000 tonnes of wood chips a year over a period of 15 years. It is a 'chicken and egg' situation: farmers are not prepared to plant coppice until there is an outlet for the wood, and a generating plant cannot operate without wood. Scandi-navian experience suggests that the demand for wood chips and other biomass products increases as production comes on stream.

Straw, which can no longer be burned in the fields of England and Wales, is a useful material as fuel and for paper making. Several countries in the EU use straw and other wastes for neighbourhood heating and electricity generation. A plant might take 28,000 tonnes (56,000 large bales) annually. Small straw-burning power stations are planned in some arable counties but farmers will expect to receive a reasonable price for baled straw. Baling and carting represent an extra cost over ploughing in, and some farmers find that the increased traffic created by this activity can cause soil structure problems.

A good deal of research is underway into the production of elephant grass (*Miscanthus*), which grows up to 3 metres in a year and can easily be harvested by machine and chopped for burning as a fuel. Like coppice wood and straw, it provides a renewable

Producing wood pellets from coppice

Coppice regrowth

source of dry matter and could retain, if not create new, jobs in the countryside.

Food and industrial crops will perhaps in the not too distant future be required again from land which is now set-aside. The population of the world was 5.3 billion in 1990 and at the lowest estimate is projected to rise to 7.6 billion by 2025. Every year 28 million tonnes more grain is needed to keep pace with population growth and in recent years annual gains have averaged no more than 15 million tonnes. The present surpluses in Europe may be no more than an historic hiccup and we may soon need to increase production again, especially of those foods which are now imported but could be grown here.

4. *Use of buildings.* It is possible to make use of redundant farm buildings, provided planning permission can be obtained. Buildings have been successfully converted for small business use,

offices and residential accommodation. As with other alternatives, much depends on location and the local planning authorities.

5. *Organic produce.* There is a specialised, if limited, market for organic produce, that is vegetables and crops grown without the use of artificial fertilisers or pesticides. Organic livestock products are also produced: milk and dairy products, lamb, beef, pork, etc. Where livestock are fed on home-grown foods, no problems arise about how they are produced. There may be difficulties if feed is imported on to the farm, as the exact origin of its constituents may not always be known.

Producers marketing foods as organic must comply with the requirements of the United Kingdom Register of Organic Food Standards (UKROFS). It is not usually possible to graft organic husbandry on to an established farm. Those wishing to supply the organic market will need to devote the whole farm to such produce and go through a conversion period before their produce may be labelled as organic.

THE TREND TO LARGER FARMS

Farm size varies considerably. Predominantly grassland livestock holdings are generally smaller than arable units, although hill sheep farms are large because of their extensive system. Farm size has been increasing steadily over several decades, especially in arable areas. There are a number of reasons for this. Most farm machinery is capable of handling large areas of crops and adding extra land makes fuller use of a machine. Machines are what an economist calls a 'lumpy input': it is necessary to own (or hire) a whole machine, so that machine size and capacity tend to dictate the area of crop. As more crops are being grown under contract to food processors, often to tight specifications, it is only the larger farms that are able to meet the requirements.

Ploughing requires on average 1.7 man hours per hectare on farms of 125 hectares or more. Farms of over 250 hectares, with larger machines and faster work rates, will require 20% less labour. Economies of scale of this order apply across all arable cropping and demonstrate one of the major reasons why farm size continues to increase.

The UK has the largest average holding size of any EU state: 67 hectares. The average for the 12 EU countries is 14 hectares. Many of these farms are uneconomic and the trend is towards amalgamation and larger farms. In France the number of farms has decreased by 600,000 in the last two decades, and there are many more large farms and fewer small ones.

A first requirement placed on farmers is for the production of cheap and efficiently produced food. Major policy will, therefore, continue to be production led. Many economists believe that this will be pursued by only a minority of farmers (who will farm a large area of land), who will be efficient and will use and adopt new technology. If the present trend continues, then some 75% of our food is likely to be produced by 10% of our farmers, much of it on contract to food producers and retailers.

This does not mean that small farms will disappear, as they will continue to form part of the countryside scene for a number of reasons. Within the EU small farmers exert a considerable, though declining, political pressure. Many EU countries have policies designed to maintain small farms through special grants in order to prevent the countryside becoming depopulated. Some small farms produce specialised commodities such as cheeses or prepared meats for a niche market. These units will continue, as in many cases it is not possible to produce such commodities on a large scale. They have 'cashed in' on their unique advantages. Many small farms in areas of natural beauty have developed successful accommodation and recreation enterprises. There are families who wish to live in the country and farm part-time whilst obtaining their main income from other sources. Such part-time farmers, who are mainly involved with livestock, maintain small farms and help to keep the infra-structure of the countryside in being. Most of the rare breeds of livestock, supported by the Rare Breeds Survival Trust, are kept on such farms. The Rare Breeds Survival Trust, founded in 1973, has as its main aim the survival of our rare and endangered breeds of British farm livestock and has been successful in conserving a number of breeds which were close to extinction.

Reference is often made to 'family farms' in terms which suggest that these are small units, but it is the size of the business which is important, and today a family farm might well be 350 to 500 hectares, with all the work carried out by the family and no employed labour other than casual help at harvest time.

THE CHANGING FARMING SCENE

It is hardly surprising that farmers in Europe and in many other developed countries find their present situations confusing. They have seen themselves change from being highly regarded producers of food in the forefront of adopting new technology to being portrayed as 'subsidised' exploiters of the animals and land through the misuse of technology. Consumers who are short of food, or where supplies only just meet needs, will not worry too much about its origin. Surpluses and plenty allow choice and make it easy to question production methods. The producer is expected to provide the quantity required, to offer wide freedom of choice and to maintain quality whilst being restricted, or perhaps denied, the methods needed to achieve these desires.

There is nothing new about having land surplus to requirements. There are plenty of examples in the UK of land which was once cultivated, often under great difficulties, to grow crops desperately needed by a hungry population. When new technology raised yields on the better land and transport allowed food to move easily, these marginal lands reverted to grass or rough grazings. Land was 'set-aside' during the agricultural depression years and reverted to poor grassland; the difference between the 1930s and the 1990s is that in the 1930s farmers received no payments for such land. One effect of paying for set-aside is that it maintains the value of land at an artificially high level. If market forces applied, land marginal to present needs would fall in value and change from arable to grass: 'Up horn, down corn'. Farms would also become larger at an even greater rate, as land would be available at lower prices to those who were able to make use of it. EU policy is designed to maintain farms and to discourage increases in farm size. Small arable farms do not have to set-aside land.

Farming and food production is, like other industries, controlled by regulations which, although necessary and desirable in many ways, also have the effect of restricting the development of production systems. The different interpretation of regulations between countries also distorts production costs and imposes unfair burdens on those who carry them out to the letter of the law.

There can be no doubt about the worldwide movements towards more liberalised trade; indeed this has been the main objective of the GATT Uruguay Round, which will exert a major influence on the reform of worldwide agricultural support systems. Support for agriculture, which is a feature of most countries, will have to be delivered in the future in such a way that trade is not unduly distorted. In the long run, environmental payments, protection for rural communities and environmental policies will need to be reconciled with open trading.

The EU has already begun to move from commodity price support to direct payments to farmers. Such payments will have to be justified as providing something more than the survival of farming businesses. The taxpayer will expect to see:

> *environmental benefits:* the conservation of wildlife and landscapes, access to the countryside and the retention of biodiversity
> *support for the rural structure*
> *food security:* this is not a problem now but would rapidly become one should shortages occur, for whatever reason

Governments are attempting to meet these criteria by recognising the need to develop environmentally integrated agriculture without compromising the need to improve productivity. Combine harvesters will still be needed.

Each country will have to decide what it means by 'sustainable' agriculture and the criteria are likely to differ, although the basic principles should be the same. Within Europe these are:

1. to sustain the basic resources of water, soil nutrients and air which will entail minimising pollution and soil erosion and protecting long-term water supplies
2. to conserve biological diversity and to make livestock and cropping systems as environmentally efficient and safe as possible. This will lead to the development of integrated crop management systems and new livestock systems which improve pest and disease resistance in plants and animals. These systems will, wherever possible, use methods of biological pest control, so reducing the dependence on the use of chemicals
3. to sustain the efficiency and competitiveness of farmers so that they are able to produce food, fibre and other products of high quality, safe and conforming to an acceptable code of animal welfare

Individual farmers will be encouraged to move towards these criteria through incentives, together with pressure from market forces, new technology and public perception. CAP funds should be switched increasingly from production and area payments to environmental and socio-economic payments from which the public can see direct benefits.

There is a strong market for high-quality, safe food and this is the greatest single advantage enjoyed by EU agriculture with a population of 375 million consumers on its doorstep.

The Agricultural Development and Advisory Service (ADAS) and institutes such as Long Ashton Research Station have done considerable research into less intensive farming methods. LEAF (Linking

CHURN ESTATES

*The farm manager
in his office*

*Outdoor suckling
sows*

Pig weaner accommodation

Sheep and lambs at summer pasture

Indoor feeding of beef cattle

Cutting lucerne for drying

Dried lucerne leaving the drier

Pea viners at work

This combine handles 500 ha of crops

Mechanised bale handling

The end result – a range of high-quality produce
(Courtesy of RASE)

Environment and Farming) aims to develop a profitable and practical farming system which will address the concerns of the consumer and meet the needs of the farmer. Farmers are beginning to adopt integrated crop management involving the optimal use of pesticides with decisions based on disease and pest thresholds, crop monitoring, diagnosis and husbandry or biological means as a method of reducing the risk of problems. Producing crops through these methods is seen by farmers and the large retailers as a more satisfactory means of meeting the needs of consumers than providing organically grown produce. Such produce would not be labelled, and everything would be produced to the Codes of Good Agricultural Practice, thus avoiding the development of a niche market. Those not reaching the required standard would have great difficulty in selling their produce. The evidence from research and practice so far available shows that these systems can be successful but they require careful and skilled management with attention to detail. There are potential savings to be made by reducing inputs of fertilisers and pesticides but penalties can be incurred from omitting or reducing key inputs. Skill is required to get the correct balance and this becomes greater as the pressure to reduce these inputs increases.

BIOTECHNOLOGY

In the production of both plants and animals there is a clear understanding that, if progress is to be made towards more sustainable agricultural systems, much more knowledge is required about the complexity of the agro-ecosystem. Strategies must be developed based on existing knowledge and modified to take into account new material as it is developed.

In the long term it may be possible to improve the efficiency of the process of photosynthesis, the means of nutrient uptake and the ways in which plants take up, and use, water. To do this requires a knowledge of the genes which control cell and plant functions and a better understanding of the internal and external factors which influence plant growth and development. In the short term some improvements can be brought about through plant breeding and the selective use of chemicals in order to improve the crop canopy so as to increase the capture of light which provides the plant with the energy it requires for photosynthesis. Another option is to exploit plant species and variety differences and select plants which use nutrients more efficiently.

Plant molecular biology offers new ways to manipulate the genetic blueprint of plants in order to influence those characteristics we find desirable. Such processes are being developed but are not, so far, widely in use. It might be possible to introduce into non-legumes the ability to 'fix' nitrogen from the air through symbiosis with bacteria. This would reduce the need for artificial sources of nitrogen.

Some plants have resistance to pests and diseases and it may be possible to transfer this naturally occurring resistance or tolerance from one plant to another so as to reduce crop losses and the need for chemical protection agents.

Breeding plants which are more digestible or more palatable will encourage animals to eat more and improve their efficiency of utilisation. Grasses, for example, are being bred with a high soluble carbohydrate content which is advantageous in silage making, where the sugars increase bacterial activity.

It is also possible to improve the keeping quality of fruit by introducing genes which slow down the ripening process. Transgenic tomatoes ripen more slowly and store far longer because they contain a gene which inhibits the formation of ethylene, which is involved in the ripening process. This approach can also be used to modify the ripening characteristics of many other fruits and may reduce the need for special methods of storage and transport.

Mankind has continually sought to improve and alter the form and function of domesticated animals, and farm animals are no exception. In recent years, as knowledge of molecular genetics has advanced, science has been able to provide new techniques to speed up this process in animals as well as in plants. Such techniques in embryology and in the transfer of genes across species boundaries open the way to introducing desirable characteristics into species and varieties which do not already possess them.

The promises of such technologies, however, are subject to value judgements which embrace ethical considerations, and these will influence not only the direction but the way in which such technologies can be developed and applied. The ethical dimension is a major issue in relation to the ways in which the promise of biotechnology can be fulfilled in the search for sustainable systems of agriculture. Care will need to be taken in producing 'new' crops or animals which, if allowed to spread naturally into the countryside, could dominate other species. Concern has also been expressed about introducing genes from other species into crop plants which, if released into the wider environment, might produce undesirable changes in wild species. Crop plants engineered to be resistant to herbicides would make weed control easier, without the risk of damage to the crop. However, if the resistance spread to related weed species then obvious problems would arise.

THE FUTURE

The farmer of the future will continue to rely on inputs of innovative technology both on the farm and in the processing and distribution of produce. Producers will also need to be closely attuned to market requirements and be prepared to alter production systems to meet specifications laid down by the market. In order to do this successfully the industry should not be placed at a disadvantage through the supply of food from other countries where regulations are ignored. New agrochemicals and biological control agents used overseas should be available in the UK and regulations should not be introduced for which there is no scientific justification.

The UK farmer has a major advantage over his international competitors in farm size and structure and in the low numbers of workers employed. The country has an equable climate well suited to growing most temperate crops and to the production of livestock. There is a wide variation in soils and climatic differences which make it necessary to choose cropping and livestock systems best suited to the location. The best UK producers of cereals, root crops and vegetables are technically equal to any found in Europe.

European agriculture will, in the short term at any rate, be reduced both in area and in the number of farmers, with a falling income and the need to move towards a market economy. Individual farmers will have to compete in a single European market and, increasingly, in a single global market with only limited protection.

Farmers will need to reduce unit costs, although this will not always imply lower input systems. Cooperation, increased scale of operations and lower machinery costs will also be important. They will have to be more careful about the impact of their farming practices on the environment and they will be offered funds to help them take appropriate measures. There will be higher standards of veterinary health, hygiene and animal welfare. They will need to use new technology in order to reduce costs and develop environmentally compatible systems which will produce high-quality, competitive and safe products. They have to do all this and run a viable business, as without financial viability, farming cannot fulfil its responsibility of custodianship for the countryside and the natural environment.

Agriculture and the food industry must achieve an understanding with society which will enable it to use all its skills to continue to deliver high-quality food through acceptable agricultural systems.

CHAPTER SEVEN

A Case Study

The changes that have taken place in UK agriculture over the past 50 years are well illustrated by looking in detail at a farm estate on the Berkshire Downs which is well documented and typical of larger arable units. Churn Estates Limited was purchased by the University of Reading in 1969 and is run as a commercial enterprise. The authors are grateful to the University for permission to draw on the very detailed records.

Churn Estates was built up by the industrialist Sir Charles Colston between 1948 and 1950 by the purchase of five farms to form one unit of 701 ha. The soils range from light downland loam over chalk through medium loam on greensand to a rich loam over chalk. These soils are suitable for early cultivation and, although the area is very exposed, have the potential to grow a wide range of crops. The farm is well supplied with essential services and has a number of good internal roads. During the 20 years before it was purchased by the University it was operated as a commercial enterprise with sporting and residential interests.

In 1950 the staff totalled 32:

    20 general farm workers
    3 shepherds
    3 gamekeepers
    6 estate staff

There was a ratio of one farm worker to 31 ha of arable land.

The bulk of the land, 620 ha, was devoted to arable crops and in 1950, besides wheat and barley, these included peas, lucerne, clover for the sheep and mustard, some of which was harvested and some ploughed in as green manure.

Tractors were in general use and a combine harvester had been introduced in 1947.

At that time the farm carried a flock of 800 ewes and five Guernsey cows to supply milk for the farm staff and their families. The three shepherds were responsible for the 800 ewes, which made a ratio of one shepherd to 266 ewes. They may also have been expected to take care of the five dairy cows.

A study of the farm enterprises illustrates the changes that have taken place and the reasons why such changes have been necessary.

Mechanisation in the early 1950s: a crawler tractor pulling three drills requiring four men

CROPS

Cereals

In the 1950s the major crop was spring-sown barley, as soil fertility was low and not capable of sustaining other cereals. The barley stubbles remained over winter for game shooters to walk over during the shooting season as at this time shooting had a major influence on the cropping programme.

Wheat was introduced in the 1960s on the more fertile areas of the farm. Couch grass was a serious weed problem through the 1960s and 1970s but was eventually brought under control through

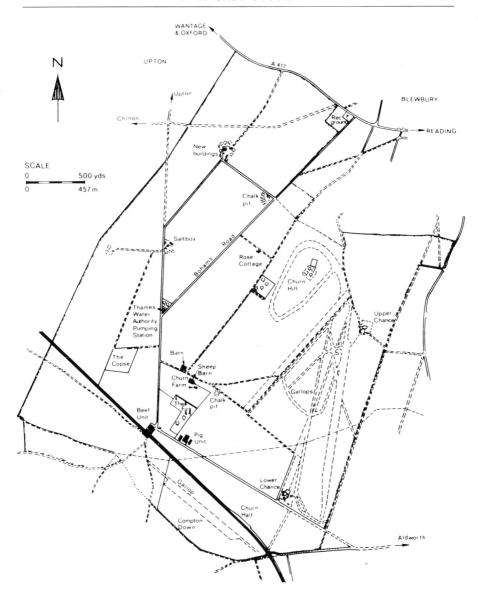

Churn Estates

cultivations (helped by larger and more powerful tractors) and
the use of gramoxone. Winter barley was grown in the 1970s
when new fungicides became available which could control leaf
diseases like Rhynchosporium, which had previously made this crop

uneconomic. Today there is a high proportion of wheat in the rotation as soil fertility has been improved, mainly through the use of slurry from the pig finishing unit.

Lucerne

This crop was introduced in the 1950s and was grown for drying. At this time there was a demand for the dried product as it provided carotene which helps to maintain a deep colour in egg yolks when added to poultry rations.

Lucerne grows well on the chalk soils at Churn and integrated with the sheep flock, providing some valuable winter and spring grazing. A light cut was taken in the first year of establishment, and then there were three years of full harvesting (3 or 4 cuts each year) before the lucerne was ploughed out for planting to wheat.

Drying ceased in the 1970s, mainly due to the increased cost of fuel (oil) and electricity and the cost of labour. Sufficient labour was no longer available to operate the three shifts needed to keep the dryer in full operation during the season as, with increased mechanisation of farm work, there was less work available on the farm at other times of the year in relation to the value of the dried product.

Synthetic carotene formulations became available, so reducing the demand for the 'natural' product.

CAP incentives also made the replacement of lucerne with cereals attractive.

Vining Peas

These are peas grown and harvested green for canning or freezing. This crop was introduced in the 1960s when there was a large increase in demand for green peas. A canning factory five miles away provided the vining service (separating the peas from the pods and the haulm) until 1968 and then a cooperative was formed with five other farms to purchase and operate two new mobile viners.

Production stopped in 1979 when the canning factory was taken over through a food industry merger which resulted in pressure to increase factory margins. Pea growers received no price increase for their crop for two years, and cereal growing was becoming more profitable again.

Dried peas were grown for some time as an alternative to vining peas but proved difficult to harvest on the stony soils and have been replaced with beans.

Oilseed Rape

This became available as an alternative break crop. New varieties acceptable to the oilseed crushers became available, making this an increasingly profitable combinable crop.

Potatoes

These were grown in the 1960s for canning by the same factory that handled the green peas. There are suitable soils on some parts of the farm and casual labour was available for lifting. At that time machinery was not available to harvest small canning potatoes.

The crop is no longer grown, as casual labour ceased to be available and cereal growing became increasingly attractive. Potatoes are grown on farms without stones so that mechanical harvesting can be carried out. The stony soil at Churn made mechanical harvesting impossible.

Sugar Beet

This was also grown but was dropped due to rather unsuitable soil types over most of the farm, as well as the increasing costs of transporting the beet to the factory at Kidderminster.

LIVESTOCK

Beef Cattle

These were introduced in 1973 as an alternative to milk production at a time when the long-term economic outlook for milk was not encouraging. Grant aid was available for beef buildings, and new varieties of forage maize became available which could be made into silage suitable for the winter feeding of beef cattle.

The beef cattle enterprise was dropped in 1986. Interest charges had increased to 18%, much more than the unit could carry. It also became difficult to harvest the forage maize for silage in the autumn and clear the ground in time to plant winter wheat. The gross margin from cereals continued to increase at this time, making them much more attractive and less risky than beef cattle production.

Pigs

A pig breeding herd was established during the 1950s using Wessex cross sows kept outdoors on the Roadnight system.

Difficult weather conditions and unsuitable stock in the late 1960s resulted in poor performance from the sows and all the stock were sold in 1968.

Pigs were re-introduced when the University purchased the farm in 1969 using hybrid sows, Large White cross Landrace, to produce meat pigs better suited to market requirements. Poor performance from this type of sow, together with bad weather, produced variable results and in 1979 an indoor system was established in converted old buildings.

The original piggery, now demolished

This system continued and in 1985 the pig finishing unit was producing such good margins that it was expanded. A fully automated computer-controlled liquid feeding system was installed, which provided the pigs with a feed three times per day. The farm breeding unit was not producing sufficient weaners for the fattening unit and it was difficult to expand it. Neighbouring farms with outdoor sow units were looking for a market for weaners so the Churn farm stopped the production of home-grown weaners and relied on purchased stock.

By 1991 increased risk of introducing diseases and the need for business stability made the purchase of weaners for fattening too risky and so outdoor sows were re-introduced.

In 1993 the 300 sows established in 1991 were increased to 600, with all the weaners fattened on the farm and none purchased. In 1993 the 600 sows produced 2.3 litters each during the year with 10 piglets born alive and 22 pigs weaned per sow per year.

MECHANISATION

As more combinable crops were grown on the farm, so the number of combine harvesters fell from three to one. Modern combines are reliable and technically efficient and have a high output. They are, however, very expensive to buy.

	Number of combines	Combinable crops (ha)	Ratio
1969	3	385	128:1
1978	2	405	202:1
1990	1	550	550:1
1993	1	538	538:1

A combine harvester requires only one driver (with relief for meals) but does need the back-up of tractors and trailers to move the grain quickly to a well-constructed and well-managed store. Stores for grain must be vermin- and bird-proof.

Tractors have changed over the past 40 years as much as private cars. They are safer, more reliable, easier to operate and far more comfortable to use, being equipped with cabs, power steering, radios and many other features designed to improve conditions for the driver.

For several decades the farm operated a workshop, employing two full-time fitters – very necessary when the grass drier and pea viners were in use. The workshop was closed in 1992, as machines are now much more reliable and tractors very sophisticated and often can be serviced only by agents with specialised equipment.

GALLOPS

A series of racehorse training gallops had been established on the eastern side of the estate in the 1920s and these were expanded in the 1950s. The well-established, close-cut sward combined with the spongy chalk soils to provide an ideal surface on which to train both flat race and steeplechase horses. These gallops are used by a number of trainers located in nearby villages such as Compton and East Ilsley.

1993

By 1993 the cropping on the farm had been simplified so that everything could be harvested by combine. Like other arable farms, Churn carries its allocation of set-aside. There are no sheep; the sows are run outdoors on 14 ha of land.

The 1993 cropping and yields were:

	Hectares	Yield t/ha
First winter wheat	152	7.0
Second winter wheat	158	6.7
Winter barley	32	6.0
Spring barley	33	5.5
Winter beans	19	3.8
Spring beans	34	3.5
Winter rape	60	3.0
Spring rape	50	2.8
Set-aside	91	
Total arable	629	
Land for sows	14	
Total farmed land	643	

The staff now totals 8: 3 arable men, 4 pigmen and 1 general maintenance man.

There is now a ratio of one man to 210 ha of arable crops, compared with one to 31 ha in 1950. It is hardly surprising that the countryside looks empty whilst it is well farmed.

In 1990 the one combine harvester handled 550 ha of combinable crops. In 1993 the compulsory set-aside of 91 ha reduced the combinable area to 538 ha. The one combine on the farm thus handled a smaller area, a very good illustration of one of the effects of set-aside in increasing overheads and using machines below their full capacity.

The other great, but invisible, change is in the records which are kept and the amount of paper work compared with the past. A well-ordered office is as essential to a profitable farm as skill with cultivations and growing and harvesting crops. The farm now employs a part-time secretary with access to modern office equipment including a computer. Detailed records of cropping, crop treatments, stock control of pesticides, livestock movement records, PAYE and many others are essential and on-going. In 1993 the farm, like others, completed Integrated Administration and Control System (IACS) forms to provide MAFF with a detailed and accurate record of all the fields, boundaries, woodland, roads and buildings. This has been described as the biggest and most comprehensive farm information gathering exercise since the Domesday Book in 1086 and was necessary in order to claim EC subsidies and grants. The eight-page Area Aid Application (IACS2) and the Field Data Sheet (IACS2A) had to be completed with a maximum margin of error of 2%, with penalties for inaccurate information.

Changes in the ways in which the Churn Farm has been run over the past 40 years illustrate how new technology, mechanisation and external factors have influenced farm policy.

Although mechanised in the 1950s, the farm carried a large staff as tractors were small and, basically, had replaced horses, with one tractor hauling one implement. Early attempts to make more use of available power included towing three corn drills behind one large crawler tractor. However, each drill needed a man to ride it and operate it, so the rig required four men. Today's modern unit of a tractor and drill, operated by one man, would sow more land in a day than the tractor with three drills.

In the 1950s the cereals were mainly spring-sown barley, relying on the fertility built up under lucerne and short-term clover leys for the sheep. Controlling weeds, especially grass weeds such as couch, was a major problem. The introduction of herbicides has made weed control easier and much more effective than traditional methods which depended on cultivations and exposure to desiccation. Cereals, especially barley, suffered from leaf diseases which can now be controlled using fungicides.

The technical changes allowed the manager of Churn Farm, like other farmers, to take full advantage of the CAP which encouraged the production of cereals, so that the farm moved towards large-scale cereal production with oilseed rape as a break crop. Everything can be harvested with a combine. Today the total yield of grain is about 2500 tonnes, much sold for human consumption, the remainder as stock feed.

The pea vining crop and the potatoes are no longer grown because of harvesting difficulties, and the processor closed the factory, an external factor which has affected some farmers in other parts of the country growing crops for processing.

The pig unit reflects the changes in attitude towards commercial pig production. The performance of the original outdoor unit was influenced by the weather: outdoor pigs are satisfactory but both the pigs and those looking after them suffer through long spells of bad weather. Continuous rain, cold and snow and long periods of hot weather all affect outdoor pig performance. So the breeding herd was housed for a period. Today outdoor pig keeping is accepted by public opinion as a 'good thing'. As less capital is involved than would be required for indoor housing, the system is more flexible and can be expanded or contracted to meet the demands of the pig cycle.

Livestock will always be more labour intensive than growing crops so the farm now carries more livestock workers than general farm workers. All must be highly competent and skilled in the operation of equipment.

The landscape has changed very little over the years. No hedges have been removed; indeed hedges were never an important feature of this open downland. Beech clumps remain, although damaged in the 1989 gales, and trees screen the farm buildings. The gallops on Churn Hill retain the old downland turf. There are four ancient monuments in the form of barrows on the farm which are under a preservation order. The Ridgeway path also forms part of the estate's southern boundary.

APPENDICES

ABBREVIATIONS AND ACRONYMS

ADAS	Agricultural Development and Advisory Service
AFRC	Agricultural and Food Research Council (since April 1994, BBSRC, Biotechnology and Biological Sciences Research Council)
AI	Artificial insemination
AONB	Area of Outstanding Natural Beauty
ATB	Agricultural Training Board
BOD	Biochemical oxygen demand
BSE	Bovine spongiform encephalopathy
BST	Bovine somatotrophin
CAP	Common Agricultural Policy
CLA	Country Landowners Association
EC	European Community
EEC	European Economic Community
EN	English Nature
ESA	Environmentally Sensitive Area
ET	Embryo transfer
EU	European Union
FAO	Food and Agricultural Organisation
FAWC	Farm Animal Welfare Council
FWAG	Farming and Wildlife Advisory Group
GATT	General Agreement on Tariffs and Trade
HGCA	Home-Grown Cereals Authority
HLCA	Hill Livestock Compensatory Allowance
IACS	Integrated Administration and Control System
LEAF	Linking Environment and Farming
LFA	Less Favoured Area
MAFF	Ministry of Agriculture, Fisheries and Food
MD	Minimal disease
NAA	Nitrate Advisory Area
NFU	National Farmers Union
NNR	National Nature Reserve
NP	National Park
NRA	National Rivers Authority
NSA	Nitrate Sensitive Area
NVZ	Nitrate Vulnerable Zone
SPA	Special Protection Area
SSSI	Site of Special Scientific Interest
USDA	United States Department of Agriculture
UKROFS	United Kingdom Register of Organic Food Standards

GLOSSARY OF TERMS

Biological control   the control of pests and parasites through the use of other organisms, often natural predators.

Biomass   the total of all living organisms in a particular region; also used to describe the total material harvested for use as an energy source or as a feed-stock for industry.

Biotechnology   the development of biological processes and products for the benefit of mankind and the environment.

Break crop   a change of crop in an arable rotation in order to help control weeds and plant diseases; oilseed rape grown in a sequence of grain crops would be a break crop.

Combinable crops   any crop which can be harvested with a combine harvester, a machine which cuts the crop, separates the seed from the straw, cleans it and carries it until collection by a suitable trailer.

Concentrates   animal feedingstuffs with a high food value relative to the volume; low in fibre and rich in protein, carbohydrates or fat. Usually supplied by compound feed manufacturers as balanced rations.

Conserved grass   grass preserved as hay or silage, used for feeding in winter.

Conformation   describes the shape of an animal and is concerned with carcass thickness and fullness.

Conservation headland   a sterile strip about one metre wide between the crop and the field boundary which prevents grasses such as sterile brome and couch from encroaching into the crop. A band of about six metres wide along the outside of the crop is left unsprayed and receives no pesticide treatment during the spring; necessary autumn treatments are permitted.

Contract growing   crops grown under contract to supply a specific outlet or to a factory for further processing; often grown to a detailed specification.

Coppice woodland   consists of shoots arising from stumps (or stools) of trees which are cut on a regular cycle. Used to supply small-diameter poles for building and fencing, also fuelwood. Creates a variable wildlife habitat.

Cultivations   working the soil prior to and during the growing of crops in order to kill weeds which have germinated.

Deficiency payment   payment to producers to make up the difference between the average market price for a commodity and the guarantee price when the market price falls below the guaranteed price.

Draft ewes   female sheep which are sold out of a flock, usually in the hills, to a lowland farm where conditions are less harsh.

ECU (European Currency Unit)   a standard unit of currency used throughout the EC for calculating commodity prices, grants, subsidies, etc. Related to the currencies of member states at variable rates.

Effluent   drainage from a cattle yard, manure heap or silage clamp which must not be allowed to pollute a water course.

Entire   a male animal which has not been castrated.

Extensive farming a system of farming using few inputs of bought-in feed or fertiliser, usually carried out over a wide area and on large farms in the hills and uplands.

Finished animal an animal, especially beef cattle, which has been carefully fattened and is ready for sale; a finished animal should produce a good-quality carcass.

Food conversion ratio the number of kilograms of food consumed by an animal required to produce a liveweight gain of one kilogram. This gives a measure of the efficiency of the animal in converting food into meat, and a small ratio indicates a high rate of efficiency.

Forage crops consumed green by livestock, e.g. grass, kale, lucerne, etc.

Gilt a young female pig which has produced no more than one litter.

Haulm the stems and leaves of corn, peas, beans, potatoes, etc, especially after harvesting.

Headage payment payment made to hill farmers based on the number of ewes or suckler cows kept on the farm.

Hefted sheep hill or mountain sheep which graze in the same area in which they were born, are not fenced and do not stray. A heft is a flock of such sheep and is sold with the farm.

Heifer a female cow, over one year old, which has not borne more than one calf. A maiden heifer is one that is still a virgin and an in-calf heifer is pregnant.

Horticulture the cultivation of fruit, vegetables, flowers and shrubs; also used to describe the commercial production of such crops on general farms.

Intensive farming a system of farming with the aim to produce the maximum number of crops in a year of high yield from the land available and to maintain a high rate of stocking for livestock.

Intervention storage under the Common Agricultural Policy Under the EC price support mechanism for agricultural produce, an Intervention Board for Agricultural Produce was set up in 1972. Its functions include licensing trade in a range of agricultural produce with countries outside the EC, intervention buying and the operation of other market support arrangements. Intervention buying or support buying is designed to ensure that farmers' returns are not unduly depressed by surplus production within the EC. When the free market price of specified commodities falls some way below the target price, the Board intervenes in the market, by purchasing and storing the produce. The commodity is subsequently resold, either within the EC or to a third country, disposed of as food aid or, in some cases, destroyed.

Lactation the period during which a female animal secretes milk.

Lairage a place where livestock are housed, especially at markets and docks or at abattoirs before slaughter.

Lodging of crops applies particularly to cereals where the crop has been flattened by wind and rain or because the stems were not able to support the grain. Also called a laid crop or a lodged crop.

Lowland farming farming on low-lying land as distinct from the hills and mountains; lowland farming is usually intensive.

Milk quotas   introduced by the EC in 1984 to reduce the production of milk and dairy products. Each farm has a fixed amount of milk which can be sold each year. Quota can be leased or purchased by one producer from another.

Notifiable disease   diseases of animals and poultry which must be reported to the police when it is suspected that an outbreak has occurred on a farm. Such notification is required under the Diseases of Animals Act 1950. Certain diseases and pests of plants must be notified to the Ministry of Agriculture, Fisheries and Food.

Photoperiodism   the effect of the length of day and night on plant flowering. Some plants are long-day, requiring 14 to 16 hours of sunlight a day to flower; short-day plants require only 8 to 9 hours of sunlight to flower. Others are day-neutral and unaffected by day length. Day length also affects the breeding season for animals, e.g. sheep.

Poaching   a term applied to soils which, when wet, are trampled by cattle and become churned up and muddy; a particular problem on heavy land which can lead to a breakdown in soil structure.

Premia payment   paid on the number of ewes qualifying for the sheep quota and calculated on the basis of the actual market price set against the EC guide price.

Residues (chemical)   very small amounts of chemicals used to control pests and diseases in plants which may remain in the harvested crop.

Rotation   a cropping system in which crops are grown in a field in a fixed annual sequence such as wheat, turnips, barley, ley (grass). Sugar beet is now substituted for the turnips. A rotation reduces the build-up of diseases and pests, helps to control weeds, improves soil fertility, spreads the risk of crop failure and allows the even distribution of labour requirements over the year.

Rumen   the first stomach of a ruminant (cattle, sheep and goats). It is a large sac, lined with a mucous membrane, in which partly chewed food is partially digested until it is regurgitated and chewed again—chewing the cud. It is then re-swallowed and passed to the second stomach, the reticulum, and so on through the digestive system.

Ruminant   an animal which chews the cud and has a complex digestive system with a four-part stomach: a rumen, reticulum, omasum and abomasum. Ruminants lack upper incisor teeth, and their complex stomach enables them to store and digest large amounts of bulky food such as grass.

Set-aside   land taken out of production in order to reduce the national and EU supply of produce, especially cereals. Such land receives a payment under the CAP reform. There are two forms of set-aside, rotational and non-rotational. Under the rotational scheme land is only eligible for set-aside once every six years so farmers have to rotate their area of set-aside around the farm using different fields each year. Under the non-rotational option farmers will be able to leave the same land in set-aside over a number of years.

Silage a conserved feed made from forage crops such as grass, kale, sugar beet tops, maize, etc, cut or harvested green and preserved in a silo in a succulent condition. Carbohydrates in the plants are fermented by bacteria into organic acids which act as preservatives. Well-made silage contains mainly lactic acid. When the sugar content of the material is low, molasses or other additives are used to aid fermentation.

Slurry a semi-fluid mixture of faeces and urine which may also include rain water and washing-down water from yards.

Steer a castrated male ox over one year old; also called a bullock.

Store animals kept at a steady rate of growth before fattening for market.

Suckler cow a cow which rears its own calf and is used for beef production as distinct from being a dairy cow for milk production.

Sustainable the application of husbandry experience and scientific knowledge of natural processes to create integrated, resource-conserving farming systems, based on respect for the people and animals involved, which reduce environmental degradation, and which promote agricultural productivity and economic viability in both the short and long term.

Upland hill and mountain areas, usually farmed extensively with sheep.

Weaners piglets which have been weaned (separated from their mother and no longer having access to mother's milk), usually at 3 to 5 weeks, but which have not reached the age of 10 weeks.

Welfare consideration for the comfort and well-being of farm animals. The Farm Animal Welfare Council has issued Codes of Practice covering the treatment and management of farm animals.

USEFUL CONTACTS

Agricultural Development and
  Advisory Service Headquarters
Oxford Spires Business Park
The Boulevard
Kidlington
OX5 1NZ   0865 842742

Agricultural Health and Safety
  Information Centre
National Agricultural Centre
Stoneleigh Park
Warwickshire
CV8 2LZ   0203 696518

Centre for Management in
  Agriculture
Farm Management Unit
University of Reading
PO Box 236
Reading
RG6 2AT   0734 875123

Country Landowners Association
16 Belgrave Square
London
SW1X 8PQ   071 235 0511

Countryside Commission for
   England
John Dower House
Crescent Place
Cheltenham
GL50 3RA   0242 521381

Countryside Council for Wales
Plas Penrhos
Ffordd Penrhos
Bangor
Gwynedd
LL57 2LQ   0248 370444

English Nature
Northminster House
Peterborough
PE1 1UA   0733 340345

Farming and Wildlife Advisory
   Group
National Agricultural Centre
Stoneleigh Park
Warwickshire
CV8 2RX   0203 696699

Food and Farming Information
   Service
National Agricultural Centre
Stoneleigh Park
Warwickshire
CV8 2LZ   0203 535 707

The Forestry Authority
Great Eastern House
Tenison Road
Cambridge
CB1 2DU   0223 314546

The Game Conservancy Trust
Fordingbridge
Hampshire
SP6 1EF   0425 652381

National Farmers Union
22 Long Acre
London
WC2E 9LY   071 331 7200

National Rivers Authority
30–34 Albert Embankment
London
SE1 7TL   071 820 0101

MAFF Hotline   0645 335577

Royal Society for the Protection of
   Birds
The Lodge
Sandy
Beds.
SG19 2DL   0767 680551

Scottish Landowners Federation
18 Abercrombie Place
Edinburgh
EH3 6TY   031 5551031

Scottish Natural Heritage
2 Anderson Place
Edinburgh
EH6 5NP   031 5549797

INDEX

A

Abattoirs, 67–68, 72
Aberdeen Angus
  beef breeds, 64
  bull, 44
Access to the countryside, 89–90
  Countryside Recreation and Access
    Groups, 89
Agricultural depression between First
    and Second World Wars, 2–3
Agricultural Expansion Plan, 3
Agricultural land, division of use, 9
Agriculture Act
  1947, 3, 18
  1957, 3–4
  1986, 8
Agriculture (Miscellaneous Provision)
    Act 1968, 61
Alternative enterprises, 90–97
Ammonia, metabolism in soil, 29
Annual price reviews, 3
Anthrax, 52
Arable farming, 16–35
  1880–1930, 18
  1939–1945, 18
  controlling production, 32–34
  effects of wartime pressures, 16–17
  factors influencing development,
    16–19
  future, 34–35
  ideal arable land, 16
  influence of technology, 19–22
  legislation, 23–27
  organic farming, 31–32
  pre-war unprofitability, 17–18
  'up corn, down horn', 18
  water supplies, 27–31
Area Aid Application (IACS2), 113
Artifical insemination, 43, 59
Attested Herds Scheme, 37
Automatic cluster removers (ACRs), 48

Ayrshire breed, 64
  dairy cow, 41, 42

B

Biochemical oxygen demand of silage
    effluent, 46
Badgers and tuberculosis, 52
Bail milking machine, 38
Barley, spring-sown, Churn Estates
    Limited, 106
Barley beef, 65–66
Battery hens, *see* Poultry production
    systems
Beef cattle, 55–69
  all-year housing, 55
  at Churn Estates Limited, 109
  average herd, 55
  future, 69
  handling, 67–68
  hill and upland, 56–59
    winter housing, 58
  price support, 68–69
  quotas, 56
  range of products, 55
Beef, lowland production, 63–67
  breeds, 66
  cereal, 65–66
  eighteen-month, 67
  from dairy herd, 64
  price support mechanisms, 63–64
  rearing calves, 64–65
  silage, 66–67
Belgian Blue, beef breeds, 64
Bio-fuels, 94
Biological control of pests, 26
Biotechnology, 102–103
Bloat, avoidance, 66
Blowflies, sheep, 61
Bovine somatotrophin (BST), use in milk
    production systems, 46–47

ABOUT THE AUTHORS

Eric Carter is a graduate of Reading University, and his distinguished career in the Agricultural Development and Advisory Service culminated in his appointment as Deputy Director General in 1975. In 1981 he became National Adviser to the Farming and Wildlife Advisory Group. A Council member of the RASE, he edits its Journal. He is a visiting lecturer at Nottingham University and a member of the advisory committee of the Centre for Agricultural Strategy at Reading University and convener of the Standing Conference on Countryside Sports. He is a Vice-President of the Institute of Biology.

Malcolm Stansfield is a native of the Craven area of Yorkshire, renowned for its dairy farming. After graduating in Agriculture from the University of Leeds, he moved to Reading for postgraduate studies and has been subsequently employed by the University as Farms Manager, Deputy Director of Farms, and Lecturer. He is currently a Senior Lecturer and Director of the Farm Management Unit. A Churchill Fellow, he has travelled widely as lecturer and consultant. He is an author and video programme presenter, and has recently been elected President of the International Farm Management Association.

FARMING PRESS BOOKS & VIDEOS

Below is a sample of the wide range of agricultural and veterinary books and videos published by Farming Press. For more information or for a free illustrated catalogue of all our publications please contact:

Farming Press Books & Videos, Wharfedale Road
Ipswich IP1 4LG, United Kingdom
Telephone (0473) 241122   Fax (0473) 240501

Farming and the Countryside   MIKE SOPER & ERIC CARTER

Traces the middle ground where farming and conservation meet in cooperation rather than confrontation.

New Hedges for the Countryside   MURRAY MACLEAN

Gives full details of hedge establishment, cultivation and maintenance for wind protection, boundaries, livestock containment and landscape appearance.

Farm Woodland Management   BLYTH, EVANS, MUTCH, SIDWELL

Covers the full range of woodland size from hedgerow to plantation with the emphasis on economic benefits allied to conservation.

Pearls in the Landscape   CHRIS PROBERT

The creation, construction, restoration and maintenance of farm and garden ponds for wildlife and countryside amenity.

Farm Livestock   GRAHAM BOATFIELD

Livestock production methods explained for those taking their first steps in agriculture.

Farm Crops   GRAHAM BOATFIELD

A basic introduction to farm crops and crop husbandry.

On the Smell of an Oily Rag   JOHN CHERRINGTON

The classic account of a farming life.

Farming Press Books & Videos is part of the Morgan-Grampian Farming Press Group which publishes a range of farming magazines: Arable Farming, Dairy Farmer, Farming News, Pig Farming, What's New in Farming. *For a specimen copy of any of these please contact the address above.*